the theory and practice of HYPNOTISM

Brian Mitchell

the theory and practice of
HYPNOTISM

**Incorporating Self-Hypnosis and
Scientific Self-Suggestion**

William J. Ousby

THORSONS PUBLISHING GROUP

First published in separate volumes as *The Theory and Practice of Hypnotism 1967* and *Self-Hypnosis and Scientific Self-Suggestion 1966*
First published as a joint edition 1990

© 1966, 1967, 1990 THORSONS PUBLISHERS LIMITED

British Library Cataloguing in Publication Data

Ousby, William J. (William Joseph)
The theory and practice of hypnotism: how to liberate and use the full potential of the unconscious mind, incorporating self-hypnosis and scientific self-suggestion.
1. Hypnotism
I. Title
154.7

ISBN 0-7225-2388-2

Published by Thorsons Publishers Limited, Wellingborough, Northamptonshire NN8 2RQ, England

Printed in Great Britain by
William Collins Sons & Co. Ltd, Glasgow

1 3 5 7 9 10 8 6 4 2

CONTENTS

PART ONE

PART TWO

PART ONE

INTRODUCTION

This is not a book about hypnosis, but is a practical Course of instruction which for some years was privately circulated. It has been revised and is now available in its present form.

The language throughout is non-technical and, in addition to comprehensive instructions, the book contains a summary of the fields in which hypnosis could have value.

Foremost amongst these would be the benefits which hypnosis could bring about through incorporation in the National Health Service, but, in putting forward this suggestion I am well aware of the critical shortage of doctors available to deal with the ever increasing number of sufferers from psychosomatic illness. This shortage would, in some measure, be alleviated by an Auxiliary Medical Register of responsible hypnotherapists. Working under the supervision of doctors they could conduct Hypnotherapy Clinics, to which overworked doctors could send tense and worried patients to be taught how to relax their minds and bodies. This recommendation of an expanded Preventive Health Service, using hypnotherapy in group treatment, is dealt with in Chapter Fifteen.

In persenting this book, and a plea for incorporation of hypnosis in the National Health Service, it is with the hope that it may make some small contribution to shortening the time before hypnosis is used more widely, and many years of illness and suffering on the part of tens of thousands of people, prevented.

10 Harley Street W.1

CHAPTER ONE

USES OF HYPNOSIS

This is not a treatise on the history of hypnotism, but a practical manual of hypnotic techniques. It is not necessary to have any particular type of personality to be a hypnotist. Any man or woman of average intelligence can learn to hypnotise others, but indefinable elements in one man's personality will enable him to become successful as an hypnotist, just as one man will become a more skilful musician than another. The old idea of an hypnotist, as a dominant personality with piercing eyes is quite fallacious. On the contrary an unobtrusive manner, and a quiet monotonous voice, is a very definite advantage when carrying out certain methods of hypnotic induction.

All the methods in this book are concerned with Hetero-hypnosis (hypnotising other people), with the exception of Chapters 13 and 14, which are devoted to Self Hypnosis.

The main difference between a hypnotist and the average individual is that the hypnotist possesses, and has the skill to employ the techniques which are contained in the following pages. Until comparatively recently practitioners of hypnotism, that is doctors and lay practitioners, were unwilling to disclose their methods, with the result that the subject is still surrounded by misconceptions.

The methods which hypnotists employ can be explained and, if carefully carried out, it is a frequent occurrence for a successful hypnotic induction to be effected by the student hypnotist at his first attempt.

At one time people believed that a hypnotist possessed some special secret. Actually there is no one secret, but there are a number of simple instructions which must be observed. If these are carried out with someone who is willing to co-operate, the hypnotic state is quite likely to follow as a natural consequence. The difference is that some people may take much longer to hypnotise than others. There are many different ways of inducing a hypnotic trance a number of which are explained later in this course.

The following instructions explain various tests employed in choosing subjects to hypnotise, how to overcome resistances to trance induction, and in short, a summary of the techniques of the professional hypnotist. It is not generally realised that there are many ways in which practical use can be made of the hypnotic techniques. Before proceeding with the instructions, a brief résumé of some of the fields in which hypnotism is employed now follows.

Therapeutic Uses

Hypnotism is now proving to be of very great value in therapeutic work. Seldom a week passes without some fresh report of successful cures being achieved by the use of hypnotic treatment. It is apparent that to engage in any therapeutic work, presupposes at least some knowledge of the elements of psychology and medicine. This is because some of the psychosomatic symptoms of a nervous individual so closely resemble the early symptoms of a more serious illness that ability to recognise suspicious symptoms is necessary.

However, in practice, the lay hypnotist will seldom meet a patient who has not already exhausted the possibilities of successful treatment on orthodox lines. If a patient is relying on the hypnotherapist for guidance, where there is any suspicion of anything of a serious nature, an examination should be made by a doctor, and the fact established that the difficulties complained of do not arise from a physical cause or, alternatively, do not respond to orthodox treatment.

Hypnotic suggestion is used in conjunction with many forms of therapeutic treatment, and, in many cases, enables a hypnotherapist to treat cases successfully when all other methods of treatment have failed. Whilst it is easy to become enthusiastic when it is realised that hypnotism has effected cures of many ailments and also that it is the only anaesthetic which has had no fatalities, it must be realised that it must not be used indiscriminately as a pain killer. It must not be forgotten that pain and worry are nature's signals indicating some problem or physical condition which may require attention. No treatment should be given without medical guidance or supervision.

Hypnoanalysis

Hypnoanalysis is the name that is given to a method of conducting what is virtually a telescoped psychoanalysis. Psychoanalysis, as many readers will be aware, came into being largely as the result of hypnotic experiments, and was used for some time as a means of discovering something of the hidden form, content and operations of the unconscious mind.

Since the beginning of the century psychoanalysis has established a sound empirical groundwork, and with other branches of medical science is making increasing use of hypnotism as a tool. The undue expectations of the early analysts in the curative powers of hypnotism were seen to have arisen out of a confusion between the means and the end. Hypnotism by itself was a tool—a means to an end—and needed insight. This has been in large measure achieved in the last fifty years. That is to say by the knowledge, skill and insight of the hypnotherapist. The power of hypnotism to correct faulty behaviour and assist in adaptation is determined by how far the inner resistances and injuries are perceived and effective measures devised for dealing with them.

As an Aid to Family, Friends and Children

There are many cases where a knowledge of hypnotism enables friends or relatives to give aid or treatment to each other. If they learn how to administer hypnotic suggestions to each other, husbands and wives, friends and relatives can mutually assist each other to sleep more soundly, to achieve increased confidence, to relax, to break bad habits, and to stop worrying. They can also help to remedy or relieve many disabilities and illnesses, particularly where there is the need to repeat suggestions regularly for a period, and the aid of a professional hypnotist is not available. Parents in particular can do much to aid their children in helping them to sleep soundly, in ridding them of nervousness and bad habits, freeing them from "examination nerves," improving concentration and memory, and thus helping them with their school work and education, and generally building up morale, but it is advised that no practical experiments are carried out until the course has been thoroughly studied.

As an Aid to Business and Professional People

A knowledge of hypnotism enables the doctor, osteopath, dental surgeon, masseur, lay practitioner, solicitor and teacher to speak with greater authority and assurance. This does not mean that they will openly employ hypnotism. One of the most important of the techniques of hypnotism is "waking suggestion," which is positively employed suggestion without any "formal" induction. "Masked" waking suggestions can be administered through the medium of general conversation, or during an interview. Many business executives, doctors, teachers and officials who deal with the public are already unconsciously using hypnotic techniques in primitive form. If they understand hypnotism they will act with greater certainty and confidence. There is little doubt that most of the outstanding leaders in politics, industry, and in many other fields have consciously or unconsciously a sound working knowledge of hypnotic techniques, and this, in large measure, is the explanation of their ability to influence and control others.

Hypnotic suggestion is frequently the means of helping people to increase the quantity and quality of their work. Artists and writers whose creative ability seems to have temporarily dried up find in hypnotic suggestion a means of re-creating inspirational moods. Politicians, actors and public speakers who have become tense, and wish to relax or to increase their confidence, also benefit from the use of hypnotic suggestion.

Self Hypnosis

It has been maintained that all hypnosis is basically self hypnosis, that is to say it is the subject's uncritical acceptance of the hynotist's suggestions which, in a large measure, bring about the trance state. There is much to support this view. The hypnotic subject does not, of course, realise that it is his unquestioning acceptance of suggestion which enables the trance state to be induced, for successful suggestion is seldom recognised as such. Suggestion subtly influences people without their knowledge.

Self suggestion often manifests itself to people in everyday life in the form of spontaneous thoughts or observations. Often it would be difficult to decide whether some thoughts could be classed as justifiable observations, or as negative self suggestions. Thoughts such as "I'll never be able to do this", or "I cannot stop smoking, however hard I try" are often potent negative self suggestions, keeping alive habits which would weaken and fade if positive suggestions were substituted.

If an individual is unaware that he is using negative suggestion he may be causing himself all manner of disabilities or ailments. Fortunately suggestion is a two edged sword, and, as self hypnosis is a concentrated form of self suggestion, those who are instructed in its use can proceed to cure the ills and ailments which negative suggestion may have caused.

Successful self suggestion succeeds because it short circuits the judgment and, in this way, gains access to the unconscious mind. The knowledge and skill to do this form an important part of the hypnotist's technique, and for this reason self hypnosis is dealt with in later chapters.

In Psychological and Psychical Research

The changes in the state of consciousness brought about through hypnotic suggestions can lead to the development of faculties which would otherwise remain dormant. Some of the remarkable experiments which are possible under hypnotic control would be of very great interest to students of psychology, and psychical research. These include:

Hyperacuity

Hyperacuity is a condition which may be produced by suggestion in many hypnotic subjects. It is a hypersensitivity of the senses. By suggesting to a hypnotic subject that any of his senses will become more acute it is possible that the efficiency of that sense may temporarily be increased, for example, a good hypnotic subject may be made to hear minute sounds or to detect things which he would not normally see or hear in waking consciousness, and which would be inaudible or not be perceived by a normal person. This hyperacuity can increase the senses of hearing, touch, smell, taste and also of vision. In the latter case the subject will have to be in a deep somnambulistic trance so that his eyes may be opened without breaking the trance. Individuals vary greatly in their responses. In some cases suggestions to render a sense more acute will have no effect, and with others the most surprising results will be obtained. Normally hyperacuity is present only when the individual is actually hypnotised, but sometimes this hypersensitivity will persist for a period after the trance as a result of post-hypnotic suggestions directing that this ability will be retained on waking.

Regression

Through hypnotic suggestion the subject is able to move backwards in time, and recover memories which normally he would be unable to recall by an act of will. By this method very early memories can be recovered. Regression in this way has very great value in the diagnostic field. This facility also applies to the recalling of dreams which would not be remembered but for the power of hypnotic suggestion to regress the hypnotised subject.

This is not a complete summary of all the fields in which hynotism can be employed. Amongst those uses not mentioned are the teaching or aiding of others to acquire proficiency in a wide variety of subjects such as learning shorthand, typing, to play musical instruments, swimming, dancing, and as an auxiliary in many professions. Instructions for the first practical steps in becoming a hypnotist are given in the following sections.

The unconscious processes governing the emotional and physical life have their roots deep in, and are nourished from the source of life itself. Contact with this deeper source of life can be achieved by means of the hypnotic and self hypnotic techniques, when allied with a sincere attempt on the part of the individual to carry out his true role in the broader scheme of life.

CHAPTER TWO

CHEVREUL'S PENDULUM

There are various tests which are used to select the people most susceptible to hypnotic suggestion. These tests are by no means infallible. Frequently those who have not responded well to the initial tests may prove later to be excellent hypnotic subjects. Carrying out these tests gives the student hypnotist an excellent opportunity of practising the technique of making suggestions.

A classic test of self suggestion which the reader can experiment with for himself was named after Chevreul, a distinguished chemist and Director of the Natural History Museum in Paris. He was reputed to be the only man of world wide fame whose centenary was celebrated in his own lifetime. He lived to the age of 103. He investigated the apparently inexplicable movements of the pendulum used by mediums and clairvoyants.

An Example of Unconscious Self Suggestion

Usually the pendulum was a ring suspended by a thread and held near a wine glass. The ring would swing, apparently of its own accord, and tap out messages on the wine glass, one for A, two for B or some such code. Chevreul proved by a series of experiments that though people could be acting in perfectly good faith, the movements of the pendulum were caused by almost imperceptible muscular movements of the hand holding the thread; in other words the pendulum's movements were caused by involuntary movements on the part of the individual holding the ring who was completely unaware of the unconscious movements of his hand.

In these cases the movements were caused by unconscious suggestion, and it is now recommended that the reader himself carries out the experiment on the following lines.

A Suggestion Experiment on Yourself

Take a small weight, to which a thread can be attached—a ring, or small key, will serve admirably. When you have tied the weight to the end of the thread, tie the other end of the thread to the end of a pencil so that it forms, as it were, a miniature fishing rod and line, the pencil being the rod, and the thread (which should be about eight inches long) forming the fishing line, with the weight suspended at the end of it. This device is known as Chevreul's Pendulum. Take a sheet of paper and on it draw a straight, bold line about six inches long. After placing the paper on the table or the floor, hold the miniature fishing line with finger and thumb at the other end to which the thread is tied, so that the weight is suspended over the line you have drawn, about one inch from the paper. Direct your gaze intently on the line, and in a short space of time the weight will, apparently *of its own accord*, begin to sway backwards and forwards following the direction of the line. It is almost uncanny, once the pendulum has got on the move, to watch its performance—it will increase the arc of its swing backwards and forwards quite briskly. Whilst it is in motion move the paper round so that the line now points in a different direction— keep your eyes steadily on the line and, in a few minutes, the pendulum will also alter its direction and will again swing along the line.

Second Stage in Experiment

When the pendulum has responded well, draw a second line at right angles to the first, hold the pendulum over these lines, at the intersection of the two, and it will be found that it will invariably travel up and down the line *on which you direct your attention*. After this has been successfully accomplished, draw a circle. It will be found that the pendulum will swing in a circle *when you direct your attention on the circle*.

If, at the first attempt the pendulum does not respond immediately, do not be discouraged. With the majority of people some movement begins within the first minute, whilst with others a number of sittings may be necessary before the facility is acquired. In cases where the pendulum does not respond this is due, either to inattention, mind wandering, or unconscious sabotage. In all cases progress will be made with patience and practice.

Some readers might feel inclined to resent the accusation of inattention or unconscious sabotage, but when we examine the mechanics underlying the behaviour of Chevreul's Pendulum, it will be appreciated that OUR UNCONSCIOUS ATTITUDE towards the experiment is the dominant factor. The movement of the pendulum is actually caused by imperceptible movements of our hands, though WE ARE QUITE UNAWARE OF THE FACT. The conscious mind is keenly intent on what is happening in the role of an observer, and until his attention is drawn to the fact is unaware of the compulsive influence which suggestion is exercising.

A Suggestion Experiment on Somebody Else

This experiment is to be carried out not only on oneself, but on others. Ask someone else to hold the pencil and instruct him to direct his gaze on the line which has been drawn on the paper. The suggestion is then put to him that the pendulum will sway along the line and, in the majority of cases it will do so. If the subject says or thinks: "It is not moving," or "I don't think it will work with me," then it will not move. This is because he has unconsciously or consciously accepted the suggestion that it will not move and the negative suggestion has become effective.

Get the subject to hold the pencil whilst standing up. See he keeps his elbow away from his side, and stands back about eighteen inches from the table. Concentrate first on one line and, when the pendulum has obeyed this suggestion, then on the other. Suggest: "It will now swing in a small circle—now the circle will grow." Then say to him: "In a few moments it is going to stop," then wait. It may take a little while, but gradually the pendulum will come to rest and hang down perfectly still. If he thinks it will move in a straight line in any desired direction, it will do so, if he thinks it will move in a large circle, a small circle, an ellipse, or that it will stand still, it will obey his instructions. The proficiency of the individual in this experiment will increase as his nerves and muscles become educated in making the imperceptible movements which cause the pendulum to move, though he is himself not consciously aware he is causing the movements

The purpose in carrying out this experiment is to demonstrate that if an idea is accepted by the unconscious mind, it automatically becomes true, also for the reader to begin practising making suggestions to other people.

CHAPTER THREE

SUGGESTIBILITY TESTS

The next step is to find someone who is willing to co-operate in further experiments. Explain to your fellow experimentor the object is to demonstrate that the more we know about suggestion, the more we are able to employ it for the benefit of others as well as ourselves.

For your own part, regard the exercises as purely experimental. Be prepared for failure or only partial success, but do not let this deter you, as the object of these preliminary experiments is to gain practical experience.

The following experiment can be tried on someone else without the necessity of an explanation. It offers an excellent illustration of the difference between theoretical and practical knowledge on the most important subject of relaxation.

Relaxation Test

To carry out this experiment, ask a friend to stand up and look straight ahead. Ask him to raise one of his arms to shoulder level. Place one of your hands under his upper arm, and the other under his hand whilst standing in front of him. His arm will now be supported in a horizontal position by your two hands. Tell him to relax the muscles of his arm, repeating the instruction several times. Then ask him if he has done so. Keep your own hands perfectly steady during this procedure. When, in response to your enquiry, he tells you his arm is relaxed, withdraw your hands suddenly. If his arm muscles have been completely relaxed, his arm will immediately drop limply to his side. If there has been only a partial relaxation, the arm will fall slowly. If there has been no relaxation the arm will remain outstretched. If your subject has failed to relax correctly, explain to him that though we may believe we know what relaxation is, in actual fact we may fail in a practical sense to achieve it. Repeat the experiment until your subject grasps the idea; you can vary the procedure by using the other arm, then both arms together, bringing both arms out in front instead of sideways.

Swaying Test

For your next test, explain first to your subject that you are now going to demonstrate how suggestion affects the imagination. Ask him to stand erect with his feet close together. Tell him to close his eyes, make his mind a blank and listen to you. Now tell him that he will be unable to stand perfectly still because he will start to sway slightly from side to side. Tell him that the harder he tries to maintain his balance, the more difficult it will become. Watch his movements and amplify your suggestions with appropriate comments such as: "Now you are swaying to the right ... and now to the left. ... Now you are swaying backwards ... and now forwards ..." etc. Keep up these suggestions for a minute or two. There is a close parallel to be drawn between this experiment, and the exercise of Chevreul's Pendulum. The muscular movements are in both cases due to suggestion.

Do not feel disappointed if your subject remained immovable. The reason for the failure may have been because the subject selected was consciously or unconsciously not co-operating, or perhaps because your suggestions were unconvincing, or some outside disturbance may have distracted his attention. There are many reasons why suggestions, both to ourselves and others, may fail from time to time. Do not be disappointed but analyse what has happened, remember the main object of your experiment at this stage is to gain experience.

Swaying Test—Second Stage

Next, ask your subject to stand upright again with his eyes closed and feet together. Stand behind him and say: "I am going to place my fingers on the back of your neck ... there!" at the same time firmly pressing your fingers on the base of his skull. Then say: "I am going to draw my finger backwards gently, and you will find yourself swaying backwards with it." Assure him that he will not fall because you will stop him as soon as he begins to sway backwards. Then very steadily and slowly draw your hand backwards, and he will, if your suggestion has been convincing, start to sway backwards. Stop him by placing your hand on his shoulder. Repeat this experiment several times.

It is better to keep your subject's attention engaged so, even if what you say is somewhat repetitive, continue to comment authoritatively on the way suggestion, playing on the imagination, influences our actions. These "explanations" play an important part in the experiments, for they provide the opportunity of planting suggestions in the subject's mind. If the average subject implicitly accepts your word that what you suggest will happen in an experiment, then, almost invariably, it will happen. If, on the other hand, he is critical or antagonistic the experiment will, in all probability, be a failure or only partially successful. Therefore, in making your suggestions, phrase what you say in such a manner as to be acceptable to the subject and not likely to arouse any unconscious resentment.

Swaying Test—Third Stage

Proceed to say something on the following lines: "The success of this experiment depends entirely on your ability to keep your mind clear—just push all other thoughts out of your mind and listen to me. I am going to place my finger tips on your temples—so—and as I draw my hands forward you will find yourself swaying forward." Whilst giving these instructions illustrate what you are saying by placing your fingers on *your own* temples, and as you say the above words—"you will find yourself swaying forward" illustrate by actually swaying forward yourself. This little illustration, if deftly executed, exercises considerable influence on the subject. Next say: "That's right, put your feet closer together. Your toes as well as your heels; stand to attention, hold your head up and look straight at me, *just balancing upright.*" Note the emphasised words; these are significant. As you say them put your hands on the subject's shoulders, and gently sway him backwards an inch or so, then bring him forward again to the upright. See that he does not move his feet, and that he does not raise himself up on his toes. Now rock him gently backwards and forwards several times telling him to let himself balance upright. The object of this is to loosen his calf muscles and see that they are not rigidly braced. When ready tell your subject to look straight at you, to keep his mind clear, and whilst you are talking, stretch out your arms towards him and place your fingers lightly on his temples. Continue talking, and at what you judge to be the right moment, or if you feel a slight forward movement, draw your hands towards you, keeping your fingers still on his temples. At the same time say: "You are coming forward, forward, forward." A slow movement and considerable practice is necessary to calculate just when, and at what rate, the hands are to be moved. You can vary this experiment if you wish by having the subject close his eyes, and keeping them closed throughout the test.

Locking Subject's Hands

For the next attempt instruct your subject to clasp his hands together. The standing position is best, but he may be seated if you wish. The palms of his hands should be pushed hard against each other, and his fingers interlaced. Now ask him to think that his hands are so tightly fastened together that he will be unable to move them. Tell him to think that his hands have become stuck together, and to keep repeating it to himself. Instruct him to look straight at you and, under no circumstances, to look away. Now place your hands outside his and press his hands together, at the same time looking at him steadily and saying: "Press them together firmer, tighter, tighter still; they are beginning to stick, they are sticking together tightly, you will not be able to get them apart; the harder you try the more impossible it will be." Then pause and pronounce firmly, "Your hands are tightly fastened together—you cannot unclasp them...." Remove your own hands from his but continue to gaze fixedly at him and continue your suggestions. Some people however hard they try will be unable to get their hands apart. If he is unable to unclasp his hands, say to him in a quiet and confident manner, "All right, stop trying, I am going to count and when I get to 'Three' you will be able to unclasp them...One, Two, Three, open them." He will then be able to open them for your earlier suggestions have been neutralised. It is much easier to remove this effect than produce it. The influence of your suggestions is likely to weaken as soon as your suggestions cease, or your subject looks away.

Armchair Test

Another conditioning test, is to tell the subject to sit in an armchair with his legs stretched out and his arms relaxed. When he is comfortably relaxed tell him he is not to move his arms or legs, and that when his eyes are closed he will find that he is unable to stand up. Then tell him impressively to close his eyes. If all these instructions are given in an authoritative manner the subject, in all probability will not be able to stand up. The loss of volitional control experienced by the subject will be commensurate with the measure with which he has accepted the instruction affecting the movement of his limbs. It is manifestly impossible to get out of the chair without establishing a new centre of gravity which would involve the movements of the limbs.

The success of these experiments depends on your ability to give the instructions with such conviction that they are accepted and believed by the subject without question.

Analysing Your Experiments

Regard these tests as experiments in suggestion which is what they are. If your experiments were only partly effective, think about what has occurred. Discuss his experience with your subject. Try and discover the causes of failure. Often they are obvious; some noises or distraction, unsteadiness in your voice, some hesitation in your manner. Sometimes it may be simply the fact that your subject did not understand your meaning, due to some slight ambiguity in speech. Discuss the matter thoroughly; find out what he thinks about the experiments—what his reactions are. Reverse the roles and get him to make the same suggestions to you. This will give you some idea of how you react to suggestion.

CHAPTER FOUR

PRE-CONDITIONS FOR HYPNOTISING

To explain how to hypnotise an individual is not difficult. To put that advice into practice is an entirely different matter. It is, in a sense, a creative work; for example, anyone can get paints, brushes and canvas, but it requires an artist to paint a picture. The hypnotist's canvas is the subject's mind. He paints with words and actions. If he uses them aright he has a hypnotised subject, and if he doesn't he fails. In the main, ninety per cent of the work is done beforehand by the hypnotist on himself, so that he may be able to adapt himself to the various situations which arise.

What Prospective Subjects Think

Consideration must be given to what is happening in the subject's mind before the attempt to hypnotise him is made. If your proposed subject is in any way uneasy, or expresses any unwillingness, it is wisest to find another subject. It is extremely unlikely that you would get any results, and there is always the possibility that an awkward or invidious situation would arise. Never lose sight of the fact that there still exists a fair amount of prejudice against hypnotism.

Subjects' Misconceptions About Hypnosis

Among the people who wish to be hypnotised will be some whose attitude towards hynotism will be found to be a mixture of fear and superstition. These are people who have either seen a crude stage presentation, or who have drawn their ideas from old wives' tales or sensational novels. Don't argue with them, merely assure them that it is a very pleasant experience which, in all probability, will help them. If they have read articles in magazines or newspapers of the successful treatment of many complaints by hypnotism, their attitude, generally speaking, will be a rational approach. If you are talking to a reasonable individual, who has some slight knowledge of the subject, put his mind at rest so that you can be assured of his intelligent co-operation. In the main, take him into your confidence as fully as possible. If later he finds that you have misled him, or have not fully explained matters, his confidence in you may be destroyed. If what you have promised, ·or said, is found to be correct, his faith in you is strengthened.

Before attempting any experiments, careful attention must be given to the attitude of the prospective subject. Has he any interest in hypnotism? How will it benefit him to be hypnotised? Does he think he can be harmed or made to look foolish or do anything against his will? Is he nervous about talking and divulging secrets? He should be reassured on these points.

Be Cautious Whom You Hypnotise

Serious loss of prestige and possible complications can arise through thoughtless experimentation. The amateur hypnotist may be called upon to show his powers. He would be wise to avoid impromptu performances, nor should he engage in any experiment with a subject on whom someone is already carrying out hypnotic work. This latter circumstance may lead to considerable confusion in the subject's mind. *Under no circumstances should any reader carry out any experiments on anyone until the entire Course has been studied.*

People You MUST NOT Hypnotise

Never, under any circumstances, attempt to hypnotise anyone suffering from epilepsy or any irresponsible
individual or anyone who shows any symptoms of being
hysterical, nor should you attempt to hypnotise a
woman with any neurotic or hysterical symptoms except in the presence of some reliable witnesses. The
complications that can arise here will be readily grasped
when it is realised that the recollections of the individual who has been hypnotised can be very vague and
hazy, but this does not in any way interfere with what
they may imagine. Thus, a hysterical patient whose
trance recollections are confused with wish fulfilment,
can quite easily cause a most invidious situation for the
hypnotist. There is no doubt the hypnotist needs more
protection from the public than the public from the
hypnotist. There are also possibilities of complications
arising where hypnotic suggestions of any inhibitions of
physical movement or function may provide a hysterical patient with a ready-made mechanism for escaping
from reality. This is something which should be borne
in mind. Unless the reader has considerable psychological knowledge it is better to avoid hysterical subjects.

People Most Easily Hypnotised

Men and women seem to be equally good as hypnotic
subjects. Generally speaking those who follow some
organised calling, such as the police, the army or the
navy, tend to be good subjects. This is because they
have already acquired the ability to form reflexes and
to obey orders.

Those who are most easily hypnotised are children
and adolescents. Bernheim found that four children

out of five could be hypnotised. From my own experience I would say the percentage is considerably higher. Younger people are more likely to obey instructions, for the commands of the parent and the teacher may have been long obeyed without question. This is precisely what is needed—obedience without any interference from the critical conscious mind. It is for this reason that the introvert character tends to be a difficult subject. He is over critical, tends to be suspicious and analyses every move. It should be remembered that in the Hypnotism Act 1952, there is a prohibition on hypnotising in public persons under the age of 21. Details of how to obtain this Act are given later.

Conditions Favourable For Inducing Hypnosis

In theory, 95 per cent of people can be hypnotised, but failure to achieve this percentage in practice arises for many reasons, including limitation of time to carry out sufficient conditioning, failure to diagnose the hidden resistances, and obscure psychological disturbances. Some of the conditions which are helpful for hypnotising are:

Fixation of attention.
Monotonous intonation of the voice.
Limitation of voluntary physical movements.
Limitation of field of voluntary consciousness.
Inhibition of all thoughts and ideas except those upon which the attention is directed.
Quietness and warm room temperature without draughts.

Pay attention to the general environment. See that the chair or couch is comfortable. See that no bright light shines directly in the eyes of your subject—if there is a strong light it is better that it shines in your face and the subject remains in the shade. The exception to this is where a bright light is actually used as a means of inducing hypnosis. Some hypnotists prefer to work in a darkened room or with a dim coloured light. An electric light bulb of 15 watt strength which fits the standard electric fitting is admirably suited for this purpose.

Your Voice and What To Say

The manner in which one speaks is all important. Use a quiet but authoritative tone of voice, which leaves no doubt that you are fully confident and know what you are doing. Whilst you are making suggestions there must be no uneasy pauses. What you are saying should flow smoothly and easily. It is wiser to memorise the phrases you are going to use so that you may speak easily and fluently when attempting an induction.

See that your subject is seated comfortably and that his clothes are not restricting his movements or that his shoes are not tight. Talk to him whilst giving him a fair amount of time to settle down. Whilst giving him instructions, you should be gaining his confidence. Don't rush things, and avoid uneasy pauses.

The Personality and Idiosyncrasies of Subject

There are now given a number of different ways of inducing a hypnotic trance. There is no one particular way which is best. One individual will adopt a method which appeals to him or suits his personality. Someone else would prefer to evolve his own particular method. The purpose for which the trance is being induced is an important factor. The personality of the subject has to be considered, and also the prestige of the hypnotist. An amateur hypnotist has a wider scope than a therapist. He can, for example, say with great emphasis:

"You cannot open your eyes." If the subject opens his eyes the hypnotist can lightly dismiss the matter and try another method, but if this happens to a therapist the loss of prestige will make further induction of the trance more difficult. Again one hypnotist will succeed in hypnotising a subject where another hypnotist has failed. The individual idiosyncrasies of the subject are also an important factor, for example, a subject with a rebellion complex will unconsciously resent a strong authoritative approach. Someone who suffers from sleeplessness is not going to respond readily to suggestions of "You are becoming sleepy." For these reasons it is necessary that the hypnotist has some knowledge of other methods. It is not suggested that the student should practise them all, but the wider his knowledge the more flexible will be his technique.

Protect Yourself Against Negative Suggestion

Be on your guard against unconscious negative suggestion when reading the following methods of hypnotising people. It is very easy to suggest to oneself that it would be impossible for something so spectacular to occur as a result of such simple actions. We can very easily miss the thing for which we are looking. When reading the following instructions, do not look for complications where they do not exist. The majority of people fail to grasp the essentials of hypnotism not because the essentials are difficult to understand, but because they are so simple that most people overlook them.

Important

Do not give any post hypnotic suggestions, or carry out any experiments until you have carefully studied the complete Course.

CHAPTER FIVE

HYPNOTISING BY FIXED GAZE

Method One

Fixation of the gaze is one method employed for hypnotising people. As the name implies, this involves gazing fixedly at an object. There are many variations of this method, some of which are given here. The reader will later probably devise variations of his own. The usual procedure is to seat the subject comfortably and take some bright object which is held in front of the subject's eyes, slightly higher than the level of the gaze and about twelve inches from his face. It is immaterial what is used as the object—a ring, the end of a silver pencil, the end of a thimble, or a light. The subject is asked to gaze steadily at the object. When the elevated position of the eyes is maintained for a short period the eye muscles will tire. This is because the eyes are pulled inwards and upwards, converging slightly, and are in an unaccustomed and strained position. This tiring, which is a physiological process, is anticipated by the hypnotist, who makes suggestions on the following lines: "Your eyes will shortly become very tired. Your eyelids will want to close," etc., etc. The subject may blink. The hypnotist will take advantage of this and comment on the fact.

The subject's eyes must be kept fixed, gazing steadily at the object. When you first notice changes in the face and the eyes, keep commenting on these changes, saying simply: "You are getting sleepier—your eyelids are getting heavier—."

To avoid needless repetition this, and the following

methods of induction, will only be described up to this light stage. Fuller and more detailed instructions for deepening the hypnotic state are given later.

Method Two

Another method of inducing hypnosis is to give the subject a small metal disc with a spot in the centre. A small piece of black cardboard with a small piece of silver paper about the size of a pea stuck in the centre will serve admirably. Place the subject comfortably sitting in a chair and get him to cup his right elbow in his left palm. In his right hand place a piece of cardboard. Have the subject direct his gaze at the piece of silver paper and tell him to concentrate his gaze upon it, and as far as possible, to exclude all thoughts. Tell him that his breathing will become deeper, and that he will notice a slight numbness in the hand that holds the card. Sit down beside him and suggest that not only will his arms become numb, but he will feel this numbness stealing over the whole of his body. Whilst you are talking watch him closely to see if his eyes, body and features are being affected by the suggestions you are making to him. When you observe any signs of this, say firmly: "Your eyes are becoming heavier and are closing," or "Your arms are becoming heavier and more tired," or: "Your breathing is becoming deeper." If his eyes do not close, give him definite instructions to close them. When they are closed instruct him to remain sitting, listening to your voice. (Continue with trance deepening method described later.)

Method Three

Another fixed gaze method which has both advantages and disadvantages is to instruct the subject to look directly at you. Tell him to look into one of your eyes.

Indicate which eye by pointing to it with your fore-finger. The reason for this is that he will find it is im-possible to look into both of your eyes at the same time. Tell him that his breathing will become deeper, and he will begin to feel drowsy, and his eyes will want to close. Pause for a while and when he blinks, which he will do, tell him that his eyes are going to close when you count up to three. Tell him that they will close just after you have said the word "Three," and that then he is simply to rest and listen to your voice. His eyes may not close immediately after you have said the word "Three," in which case regard him steadily as there may be a slight pause between you having said "Three" and his eyes closing.

As a preparation to make this method of fixed gaze technique more effective, it is advisable to practise look-ing at a spot on the wall or in a mirror to strengthen your eyes against blinking.

Do not look directly into the subject's eyes, but direct your gaze in between them, at the bridge of the nose.

How To Avoid Unconsciously Hypnotising Yourself

Be on your guard against being hypnotised yourself.* This is possible when using this direct-gaze method and you are looking into the eyes of the subject. If you feel the onset of any trance, act decisively and without any hesitation. Immediately raise your hands and, with your fingers, firmly close your subject's eyelids. Whilst doing this say with firmness: "Rest, keep your eyes closed and listen to me . . ." shake off your own drowsi-ness and proceed with the trance deepening material given later.

* See *Self-Hypnosis and Scientific Self-Suggestion*, W. J. Ousby.

Method Four

An excellent method is to tell your subject to fix his gaze on some object and to follow closely your instructions. You then tell him that when you count "One," he will close his eyes, and when you count "Two," he will open them, and when you count "Three," he will close them, and on "Four," he will open them, and that he will continue to close his eyes on the odd numbers and open them on the even numbers. Inform him that as you continue to count he will find that his eyelids become heavier, that he will begin to feel drowsy. Tell him he will experience an increasing resistance to opening his eyes, which will grow so strong that in a short time he will be unable to open them, and when this occurs he is not to worry at all about it, but is to remain relaxed and continue to listen to you.

You need not give him any indication as to how long this will be, but you can, if you wish, say that by the time you have reached twenty his eyelids will have become heavy. This will be left to the reader's discretion, and his ability to judge matters of this nature will improve with experience.

Lengthening Pause After Odd Numbers

When you start to count, let the pause following the odd numbers be longer than that following the even numbers. There is no need to be diffident about this, but firmly make a longer pause after the "One," than after the "Two." The result of this is that the subject's eyes are closed for a longer period than they are open. Do not break the rhythm which you will employ in the counting as this should convey a smooth feeling of rhythm. This will prevent any tenseness and uncertainty, which are precisely the things to avoid. This method will lend itself to comments which you may make to amplify your suggestions. If the subject does not respond fairly easily, for example, you might employ something on the following lines:

"19. . . . 20 . 21. . . . You are feeling very comfortable. 22 . 23. . . . It is very pleasant just resting. 24 . 25. . . . Your eyes are getting heavier and heavier. 26 . 27. . . . It's becoming more and more of an effort, they're getting heavier and heavier, . . . becoming too much of an effort. They are getting so heavy that you will find that you cannot open them, and it is much more pleasant just to sit resting, because your eyelids have become so heavy that all you want to do is to rest." It will be noted that all comments are made on the odd numbers, whilst the subject's eyes are closed, and continue with trance deepening material given later.

Method Five

For this method use a blue electric light bulb, preferably focusing it on a small spot on the ceiling, with the rest of the room in subdued light. Make sure that the lighted spot can be seen easily by the subject, without effort. He is instructed to gaze at this blue spot of light while "sleep" suggestions on the lines dealt with later are made to him. It is interesting to note that some years ago a Government Bulletin commented on the fact that glass painters using cobalt blue sometimes fall asleep at their easels. This can be regarded as definite evidence that sleep or trance brought on by gazing at blue light is not entirely dependent on the suggestions employed.

CHAPTER SIX

ADDITIONAL HYPNOTISING TECHNIQUES

Method Six

Another method of inducing hypnosis is to seat the subject in a chair and give him the following instructions. "I want you to close your eyes. In a few moments I am going to place my finger in the centre of your forehead." After you have made general suggestions of drowsiness and heaviness of the eyes, place your forefinger gently on the centre of his forehead. Continue your instructions and suggestions on these lines: "Although your eyes are closed, I want you to direct them so that you are looking where my finger touches your forehead. Continue to look there. As you do so your breathing will get deeper." (See further instructions later.)

Method Seven

Dr. Esdaile's method was carried out in a darkened room. After the subject had been instructed to close his eyes and to relax either in a sitting or a lying position, Dr. Esdaile used to make slow passes with his hands over the body from head to feet, without touching his subject. What may be the value of the methods which make use of passes, the reader must decide for himself when he has more practical experience. There is much evidence to show that they are capable of influencing the subject. These methods were described either as "passes with contact," or "passes without contact." In the former case the hypnotist actually touches the body or limbs of the individual as he makes the pass, and in the other the passes are made without the hands actually touching the body. In these latter passes, the hands move within three or four inches of the subject's body. Early mesmerists and hypnotists used to make these passes with magnets. The results they achieved were undoubtedly due to suggestion. It is impossible to state to what extent suggestion is responsible for the result produced where the methods of mesmeric passes are used. Those who use these methods claim a deeper trance is possible by this means, but very often they lose sight of the fact that, if the same period of time were spent in inducing a trance by verbal suggestion, an equally deep trance would probably be induced. It is prudent, in speaking of a subject like hypnotism in which there are so many variable and unknown factors, to avoid dogmatism.

Whatever may be thought of Dr. Esdaile's hypnotic techniques, during the last century he performed some hundreds of surgical operations in India in which hypnotic suggestion was the only anaesthetic used.

Method Eight [Arm Levitation Experiment]

Having instructed your subject to sit down, without any attempt at formal induction explain that you are about to carry out a further experiment. Direct him to sit relaxed and easy in his chair and to place his hands on his knees. Tell him, by using suggestion, that you will make him feel that one arm has become lighter than the other. Spread out his fingers and let his hands rest on his knees, then say to him something on the following lines:

"I want you to look straight ahead, to go on breathing normally. Don't try to think of what I am saying, but just look at—(indicate a spot at eye level ahead of the subject)—whilst I am talking you will notice that your breathing becomes deeper. Take no notice of this, but continue to look at this spot ahead. You will also be conscious of the weight of your body. You will feel the chair where you are resting on it. You will become conscious of your clothes touching you, of your tongue in your mouth, and of your eyes feeling rather heavy. Your eyes will not close, but your breathing will become deeper. Do not think about what I am saying but simply listen to my voice. Do not think whilst I talk, but your right hand will shortly feel different from your left. There is a difference in the sensations—the left hand is feeling heavier and you have a strange feeling in your right hand. It will seem to you as though one hand is pressing down and the other is rising. In a few moments you will feel one of the fingers of your right hand will move. Do not think about it. It may be some minutes before this happens, but simply go on resting and listen to my voice. You will feel a sensation as though your right hand is going to rise up in the air, like a balloon. It will rise slowly as though it is lighter than air. You will notice that your breathing has become deeper. Push all thoughts out of your mind and simply listen to my voice." Whilst you are talking, observe your subject closely. You will probably notice a twitch or movement of one of the fingers. If this occurs, comment on it as follows:

"Disregard any movement of your hand. Do not think about it. It is important that you do not think but simply listen to my voice. Your part in this experiment is simply to listen to my voice and look ahead. All the time your left hand is growing heavier. Your right hand has an irresistible desire to move upward. You will feel the sensation in the muscles not only of your arm but your shoulder, and slowly the arm is starting to rise."

(In some subjects the movement will be imperceptible, and cannot be seen if you are looking at it directly from above, but can best be seen from the side. This should be watched very closely, as the fact should be allowed for that there may be an appreciable time lag between the suggestion being made and being acted upon.) Continue suggestions with: "There is a definite difference in the muscular tensions which are now controlling your arms. The muscles that are raising your arm are active without your wish, without your conscious control, and are now starting to raise your arm without any reference to what you feel, or what you think. You are merely an observer sitting quietly in the chair. Your breathing is deeper than usual and one arm is pressing heavily down on your left leg. It feels like a lump of lead, and your right arm feels as though it didn't belong to you, rising slowly, the whole of the time." This type of suggestion is continued until the arm moves, which it will in about three out of five people. If your subject's arm shows no sign of rising after about 15 minutes, tell him to rest—to close his eyes and forget all about his arms, and simply rest. Without disturbing him, tell him you were conducting a test—that it doesn't mean he is a good or bad subject—and to dismiss the matter from his mind and listen to your voice. Continue with trance deepening talk which is given later.

Method Nine [Diplomatic Approach to Difficult Subjects]

There are many individuals who have an unconscious resistance to being hypnotised, and with some of these people the following method will often succeed.

Some individuals may have a rebellion complex against authority or resent taking any form of orders from other people. Others may resist inductions because in dealing with nervous or emotional difficulties they may, by effort of will power over a long period, have built up a habit of self sufficiency or an attitude of independence.

Hypnotism can sometimes be successfully achieved with people of this nature by couching your suggestions in such a way as to challenge their self sufficiency or independence and pride. Appeals to pride can be made by telling this type of subject that the ability to be hypnotised depends on the intelligence possessed, and requires some power of concentration. The strategy is to challenge the subject's ideas of his ability to perform the tests and canalise his interest and endeavours. For instance, instead of telling him that his arm will get stiff and rigid, explain to him that if all intruding thoughts can be successfully inhibited, any suggestions made by the subject to himself become operative. Say to him: "Now I would like to see if you can make your arm rigid by the time I count ten. I want to see if you can concentrate sufficiently on the idea and make your arm so stiff that you will be unable to bend it." Once these contrary subjects have been successfully "misdirected," they can be influenced by the phrasing of suggestions in the above manner. Phrase all the suggestions in such a way as to make the subject feel that his power of concentration and ability to control his thoughts are being challenged.

Method Ten

Another method of inducing hypnosis featuring deep breathing, was widely used by some of the hypnotists in the last century. You can employ this method by following the instructions now given.

The subject is seated comfortably with legs stretched out, arms relaxed, head resting backward, and he is asked to take a deep breath, and addressed on lines similar to the following:

"That is right, now a deep breath this time—that is right, breathe in deeply—deeper—just hold it for a moment and then breathe out. I want you to listen to me and continue breathing in deeply as I say the words IN then OUT."

The suggestions are continued on the following lines: "Your arms and legs are getting heavy. The whole of your body is feeling heavier. Now close your eyes. Your head is feeling light and you may feel a little dizzy and detached." As the subject continues to breathe deeply the amount of oxygen in his blood stream is increased which produces a detached, hazy state of mind. The reader may prove this for himself by experimenting. Hypnotic suggestions are continued on the following lines. "Do not take notice of any noises. Just listen to my voice. Nothing is going to disturb you, you are just resting comfortably. Going further and further away into a deep, sound sleep."

CHAPTER SEVEN

SLEEP TO HYPNOSIS AND INSTANTANEOUS HYPNOSIS

It should be noted that to make any suggestions to a sleeping subject which would be resented by him if he were fully conscious, will bring into operation a resistance, and not only will the suggestions be ineffective, but the subject will in all probability wake up. This method would obviously not be used without the prior consent of the individual concerned, excepting of course under unusual circumstances, such as parents possessing some psychological knowledge and wishing to cure a child of some bad habit such as bed wetting.

Method of Operation

Do not begin to operate this method until the subject has been soundly asleep for at least an hour-and-a-half. If the subject is not used to you being in the room whilst he is asleep it is better if the induction is spaced over a period of a week or more. For the first approach, content yourself by merely entering the room and sitting for fifteen minutes or so at some distance from the bed in which the subject is sleeping. Do absolutely nothing. Content yourself for the first few sessions by carrying out the same procedure, but each time approaching nearer to where the subject is sleeping. If the approach you are making is slow and gradual, in a short time you should be able to sit on the bed of the sleeper without in any way disturbing him. When the subject is not roused from his sleep condition by your presence, you can finally address him in a quiet, low voice, or touch him without awakening him. The purpose of this slow approach is to accustom him to the slight sounds you will make by breathing, and moving, and so your presence does not disturb him. Under ordinary circumstances any unfamiliar sound or smell, such as a smell of fire, or a stranger entering the bedroom, would arouse the individual immediately. When the point is arrived at, in which the individual can be addressed in a quiet low voice, the required suggestions can be put that he is going to do as you suggest, .that he will be more confident, and is going to lose any bad habits. This method is especially suitable for a mother or nurse to use with children.

Method Twelve (Auditory Method)

There are a wide variety of methods which employ the sense of hearing. The basis of this method is monotony—this monotonous stimulation aided by suggestion often succeeds where other methods fail. The tick of a clock or a metronome, may be used. It is preferable that the tick should be slow. Suggestions may be employed at the same time so that the hypnotist's spoken suggestions and the ticks are both being heard simultaneously. Another method is to instruct the subject to imagine that the ticks are words, saying, for example, "You—are—going—to—sleep, you—are—going—to—sleep," so that they form a regular pattern.

Instantaneous Method

Sometimes a hypnotist may be seen to carry out a very rapid hypnotic induction. The induction may take place in one second, appearing to be instantaneous, and to the uninitiated seemingly bordering on magic.

Post Hypnotic Suggestion

These ultra rapid inductions may be brought about in two separate ways. In the first way the subject has been previously hypnotised, and a post hypnotic suggestion has been made to him that he will instantly pass into a hypnotic trance again at a given cue from the hypnotist. For example the hypnotist may, when the subject is hypnotised, tell him "In a few moments I am going to wake you, and afterwards if I say the word 'sleep' to you, you will immediately go into a hypnotic trance."

If the hypnotist after waking the subject, approaches him and says "sleep" the subject will immediately pass into a trance.

The hypnotic induction takes place instantaneously and is very spectacular, but in actual fact the same effect could be produced with the same subject simply by saying to him: "When I snap my fingers you will go fast asleep." If this were done, he would go into a trance just as rapidly. The whole secret of this is to choose a good hypnotic subject who has previously been hypnotised and who, in consequence of this, will pass again into a trance very quickly.

Spontaneous Somnambulists

In addition to the above method, a very rapid induction can be carried out on certain people who have never been previously hypnotised. These are a certain type of person who were described by Binet as Spontaneous Somnambulists. The triggering off of the trance is dependent on the skill and technique of the hypnotist.

Whilst in this Course I have advocated only conservative methods of hypnotic induction, I am, for record purposes giving the following description of this method of hypnotic induction, on the lines which it used to be performed by stage hypnotists, when they gave public demonstrations of hypnotism for entertainment. Quite rightly these demonstrations were banned by an Act of Parliament.

The hypnotist usually had his subject (perhaps victim would be a better word), close his eyes and stand stiffly to attention. Then, making a sudden noise, either by shouting or clapping his hands together, he swayed him rapidly backwards and laid him flat on the ground. The shock of the sudden noise, the closing of the eyes, the sudden movement backwards, plus the hypnotist's suggestions, all aided in disorientating the subject. From the point of view of a showman this type of induction was impressive but, it was not only a breach of good taste, but also a betrayal of the confidence placed in the hypnotist by the unsuspecting volunteer.

Drug Methods

A number of different drugs are used to produce changes in states of consciousness. Some of these states resemble hypnosis, but none are identical with hypnosis produced by the methods explained in this Course. The administration of most drugs necessitates medical knowledge and trance induction by these means does not come within the scope of this work.

Other Methods

It is reported that hypnosis can be produced by pressure on certain nerves, veins and arteries. There is no doubt that this is so, but it is doubtful whether the hypnotic state is attained as a direct result of these physical manipulations, or whether an intermediate submissive state is produced, from which the transition to the hypnotic trance is effected by forceful suggestion.

These physical means will be known to some physicians but in view of the attendant hazards of such methods, it is better they are disregarded, they are reported here simply to record them and to advise any students of the subject who may have heard of them not to be so ill advised as to attempt to experiment with them.

There are also some mechanical devices which are used as a means of inducing hypnosis. Among these are revolving discs, mirrors, artificial eyes and photographs of a hypnotist's eyes, but all of these visual methods have the very serious disadvantage of ceasing to be operative at the most vital and critical point in the induction which is, of course, when the subject closes his eyes.

There is no doubt that the soundest method of hypnotising a subject is a hypnotic induction. One of the author's hypnotic inductions on record and on tape recording is in regular use as a hypnotic conditioning method by many students of hypnosis and self hypnosis.

CHAPTER EIGHT

DEEPENING HYPNOTIC STATE

One of the most difficult tasks of the hypnotist is to determine the depth of hypnosis which he has produced in his subject. During the early stages of the induction, when the subject still has his eyes open, any dilation of the pupils or vacant look can be noted as disorientation takes place, but when the eyes are closed these clear and unmistakable signs are lacking.

Assessing Depth of Hypnotic State

The face in some people undergoes a distinct change as a somnambulistic and waxlike appearance is assumed. There are a number of reflex actions which take place such as fluttering of the eyelids, swallowing, twitching of the fingers and hands, and with some the face grows pale and the rate and depth of breathing often alters. There are frowns, blinks and other spasmodic movements which may be made by the subject, but to interpret what these denote is by no means an easy matter. Each individual under hypnosis reacts in an entirely different manner. The ability to judge the depth of trance is an ability which is developed by experience.

There are tests for gauging the depth of the hypnotic state, for example, telling your subject that his arm, without any volition on his part, will rise into the air, or, alternatively, that he is unable to get up from his chair or open his eyes. The degree in which your suggestions have been effective or partially effective can easily be seen, and are a clear indication of how deeply your subject is hypnotised.

Hypnotic Conditioning

It should be borne in mind that any successful test or experiment is, in itself, a form of hypnotic conditioning. For example, if the hypnotist holds the subject's arm rigidly sideways from his shoulder, and informs him that it will stay in this position, and the arm remains rigidly in this position, then, not only is it a test but also it pre-disposes the subject to accept the next suggestion.

When, by the breathing and general appearance of the subject, you judge that your suggestions have, in some measure been effective, you may proceed to carry out tests to ascertain and increase the depth of trance.

Rigid Arm Test

Take hold of the subject's arm and pull it out gently from the shoulder until it is fully extended. Give it a gentle shake whilst it is fully extended, as though implying by the movement that you wish it to remain stiffly extended. To amplify this point, if you raise the arm and suddenly let it go, it will, in all probability, drop, but if you raise the arm and support it for some seconds and firmly place it in an extended position, as though you expect it to stay there, then gently withdraw your hands, leaving it in that position, it will in all probability, remain so. There are subtle distinctions in the ways of handling, touching and moving people about, which can only be acquired by experience and shrewd observation. If, in response to this test, the subject's arm remains extended, you can firmly suggest to him that it is becoming fixed in this position and that, try as he may, he will be unable to put his arm down. Continue with these suggestions and, in all probability, he will be unable to do so. Let him try for five or ten seconds and then gently tell him that when you touch his arm it can be lowered. Take hold of his hand and, with your free hand, stroke his arm gently, lowering the rigid limb, at the same time saying: "The muscles in your arm are becoming limp and relaxed, and your arm will become perfectly normal and you can lower it quite easily."

Eye Closure Test

From this initial test you can then proceed to the suggestion of eye-closure. Say to your subject: "Your eyes are tightly closed. The lids are becoming tightly stuck together. In a few moments I am going to ask you to try to open them, but you will find that this is impossible. The harder you try, the more tightly closed they will become." Repeat these suggestions for a short time and then request the subject to try to open his eyes. When he has made an attempt for a short time, tell him to cease all effort and to relax and to go on resting. Follow this test up by the suggestion that he has become tightly stuck to the chair in which he is sitting, that his feet have become stuck to the floor, and he is unable to move the muscles in his legs, that the greater his efforts, the more tightly he will be held in the chair, as though he were pressed down by an invisible weight. Then ask him to try to stand. Continue your verbal suggestion, commenting on his inability to rise while he tries to do so. After he has tried and failed, tell him to relax and to listen to your voice. You may then inform him that he can speak without in any way disrupting his trance state. Ask him to start counting, but tell him that he will be unable to count beyond ten. In a large number of cases this will be so.

Conditioning By Hypnotic Sleep Walking

Return again to the test of being unable to get up from the chair. Repeat this test and when it has again been demonstrated to the subject that your suggestions have proved effective, instruct him to cease his efforts and relax. Then tell him that when you clap your hands together he will be able to stand up, and that you will take him by the arm and he will walk with you, and that he will grow sleepier with each step he takes. Then clap your hands and grasp him by the arm firmly and continue repeating your suggestions whilst you walk him for about a dozen paces or so and instruct him to stand still. Continue your suggestions that he will grow sleepier and sleepier. This conditioning deepens the trance.

As explained, the trance condition is deepened a little with each test. It must not, however, be assumed that the performance of a series of experiments will produce a hypnotised subject. Many subjects will act as though they were hypnotised and will carry out actions suggested to them, though, in actual fact, they are not deeply hypnotised. They will act a part because they feel it too much of an effort to resist the hypnotist's commands. It should be remembered that they wish to be hypnotised so that they may later gain the benefits of hypnotic suggestion. This compliance, if followed out, will lead to a deepening of the trance, but it should not be assumed that every subject who obeys commands is hypnotised. No two subjects ever act alike. The reader must use his own judgment in determining the depth of trance or, for that matter, whether his subject is hypnotised or not. This he can gauge from the reactions of the subject to his commands or to the tests. Generally speaking, there will be an appreciable pause before commands are carried out—often five or ten seconds' duration. The hypnotised subject has the appearance of heaviness and lethargy which would be hard to simulate. Once seen, the general characteristics are easily recognised and unmistakable. The reader, after a little experience, will choose and probably devise his own tests. By noting the reactions of various subjects on whom the tests are performed he will, in a very short time, be able to form an accurate opinion as to how deeply his subjects are effected by hypnosis.

Getting Subjects to Speak

If a subject is spoken to he will normally reply. If he does not do so, he may be told that he can speak and be asked to repeat a few words after the hypnotist, after which he can be asked questions. If any of the questions bear on matters which would render him uncomfortable, he will probably wake up. The voice of the hypnotised subject is characterised by a peculiar, dull flat tone, of a lower volume than his ordinary voice, sometimes it is almost inaudible. His general bearing is of lethargy, but this again cannot be taken as a guide for all subjects.

Caution on Demonstration

It is important when carrying out demonstrations to avoid causing a subject to perform any actions which are inimical to his dignity, or are, in any way, in bad taste. Non-observance of these points would not only break faith with your subject who has had sufficient confidence in you to place himself in your hands but will also alienate the more sensitive witnesses to your demonstration.

CHAPTER NINE

"INFORMAL" HYPNOSIS

The method of inducing a trance and deepening it simply by talking has many advantages. It has been called the "informal method," whilst the more active methods of test and experiments were given the name of "formal" hypnosis. This so-called informal hypnosis has many advantages in general medical practice. The prestige of the practitioner is likely to suffer reverses in practicing hypnotism where he fails to hypnotise a subject. The *British Medical Journal* as long ago as 19th August, 1949, in advocating the wider use of hypnotism among doctors wrote: "The technique of inducing the hypnotic state consists in telling the subject with the greatest conviction and impressiveness something that is not strictly true—for instance, that his limbs are feeling heavy, his lids drop, and he is becoming sleepy. Such things are said, and have to be said, in the hope that their saying will make them come true. Certain temperaments will find actions of this kind either antipathetic or ridiculous, and the technique cannot then be carried through with the inner certainty and self-assurance which are imperative for success." A skilful technique can avoid this apparent obstacle. By the use of purely verbal inductions a hypnotic subject need not be given the opportunity of seeing whether he can disobey the hypnotist's commands or instructions, and, in consequence of this, his views of how far he has, or has not, been affected hypnotically are likely to be unclear. Therapeutic suggestion can be very effectively administered while the subject is in this light or "informal" state of hypnosis. In many cases all that is necessary for successful treatment is the achievement of this light state of hypnosis.

Alteration in "Time Sense" of Subject

When you are speaking with the object of increasing the depth of trance, let your voice grow lower and lower until the volume is a little less than a whisper. Make frequent pauses. Let there be plenty of time for your subject to react to your suggestions. If you proceed too rapidly you will fail. Time must be given for a suggestion to register. Remember that usually the deeper the hypnotic state the longer will it take for your subject to respond. It is one of the characteristics of the hypnotic state that time values alter. If your suggestions follow each other rapidly, before the subject has had time to act on, or register one suggestion, you will be speaking to him of the next. You will, in effect, be cancelling out your own suggestions. There is another reason why plenty of time should be allowed for your suggestions to sink in. This is because the hypnotic subject will easily become confused if two ideas are introduced at the same time. He can only keep his attention on one idea, and is likely to become uneasy, disturbed or break the trance if you introduce too many ideas. Another reason for speaking slowly is that by inducing drowsiness and sleepiness you wish the subject's mind to work slowly. To achieve this effect you must speak slowly, quietly, and in a low voice, otherwise you are likely to keep his mind brisk and alert.

Deepening Hypnotic State

The light hypnotic state may be not very far removed from the ordinary waking state, but can be deepened merely by talking. These are the lines on which the talk should be based:

"You are sitting comfortably in your chair doing nothing but resting. You will hear my voice speaking to you all the time, but it will not disturb you. You will find as you sit there, that your mind is becoming sleepier. You will not try to think about what I am saying to you, but you will hear everything. As I talk you will find the heavy feeling in your arms and legs increases. With each breath you take you are slowly sinking down, sleepier and sleepier—One part of your mind is already asleep, but you will continue to hear everything I say. Your mental condition is one of quiet rest. You will shortly notice a numbness in your hands and feet. This numbness will start to creep up your arms and legs, until all your body feels numb, but it will not disturb you or make you uneasy. All you will want to do is to go on sinking down, getting sleepier and sleepier. Don't argue or reason with yourself or worry about anything. You are resting quietly, peacefully, and nothing will disturb you. The reason that we are doing this is that the suggestions I will make to you will help you. You will find this feeling of rest, of being drowsy, of being asleep and awake at the same time becomes more pleasant as time goes on. It is just as though you were sinking down quietly and peacefully into a deep, deep sleep, where nothing will worry you, nothing will disturb you—and all you will want to do is to go on resting and getting sleepier and sleepier. As you get sleepier, you will find that your breathing becomes deeper. Take no notice of this but continue to rest. Any noises which occur will seem a long way off and will not interest you at all. You will not be interested in anything except rest. You are getting sleepier and sleepier. You will notice that your body is relaxed and there is no tension present now in your body, your arms or your legs. You are beginning to learn how to "let go" completely, to sink down into a deep, deep sleep. Soon you will begin to feel very comfortable, warm, just as though you were sitting comfortably in front of a fire and feeling too tired to bother about anything except sinking down and going further and further away into a deep, sound sleep."

"You may feel a little dizzy or dreamy whilst I am talking, or my voice may seem to fade away at times, but you will take no notice of this for steadily and quietly you are sinking down sleepier and sleepier."

The reader is advised to write out and memorise some trance deepening material of the above nature, so that he may be ready to fluently make suggestions calculated to deepen the trance states he produces in his subjects.

CHAPTER TEN

HYPNOTIC DEMONSTRATIONS

There are two ways in which a hypnotic trance may be deepened. One is by "talking sleep," to the subject and the other is by having him perform a number of conditioning actions. Generally speaking the best technique should be built up from a combination of both these methods.

Some years ago excellent examples of hypnotic conditioning could be seen at public performances of hypnotic demonstrations at music halls by professional hypnotists.

Hypnotism Act 1952

These public performances of hypnotism for purposes of entertainment were prohibited by the Hypnotism Act of 1952. A copy of this Act is obtainable from Her Majesty's Stationery Office.

Stage Hypnotism

Various procedures were followed by the stage hypnotists; for example volunteers would be invited to come on to the stage to act as subjects. When the hypnotist had a sufficient number of volunteers he would begin the process of finding the best subjects. He would probably begin with some tests such as having the group as a whole clasp their hands together, and then, with great emphasis, inform them that their hands had become locked together and could not be unclasped. A few of the group would find that they could not unclasp their hands and would be noted as prospective subjects.

This was followed by a routine of relaxation or a series of tests on the lines of those already explained in earlier Sections. Those who responded well to the hypnotic suggestions were then given more attention, and the others disregarded or dismissed.

The stage hypnotist having, by means of these tests, located a group of the most susceptible of his volunteers, proceeded to have them carry out a further series of actions which deepened the hypnotic state. The antics which the volunteers were made to perform included being rooted to the floor—playing imaginary instruments — conducting imaginary orchestras — being attacked by swarms of bees—being intoxicated by drinking water—imagining they were babies and crying for their mothers—being rendered cataleptic and being sat upon or stood upon by the hypnotist, together with whatever actions the fertile imagination of the entertainer could devise to amuse his audience. Though some of these performances were vulgar and in the worst possible taste, they nevertheless presented an excellent opportunity of seeing the various stages or depths of the hypnotic state.

Indications of Depth of Hypnotic State

The following list sets out the reactions of the subject and is a general guide for indicating the progression of the depth of trance attained, but the reactions of individuals vary widely.

1 Disregard of surroundings and full attention on hypnotist.
2 Physical ease and relaxation.
3 Involuntary blinking of eyelids.
4 Swallowing reflex.
5 Closing of eyes (of own accord or by suggestion).
6 Complete physical relaxation.

7 Involuntary deep breathing.
8 Inability to open eyes, inability to unclasp hands when asked to try.
9 Inability to move limbs or get up from chair when asked to try.
10 Loss of memory in trance.
11 A paralysis of vocal chords (induced by suggestion).
12 Analgesia in trance induced by suggestion (insensibility to pain).
13 On awakening simple post-hypnotic suggestions will be carried out.
14 Trunk catalepsy can be produced.
15 Auditory hallucinations in trance.
16 Post-hypnotic amnesia (loss of memory of incidents in trance).
17 Ridiculous post-hypnotic suggestions will be carried out.
18 Post-hypnotic analgesia.
19 Can open eyes and not break trance.
20 Visual hallucinations in trance.
21 Post-hypnotic auditory hallucinations.
22 Post-hypnotic visual hallucinations.
23 Complete somnambulism.

The professional entertainer had many advantages over the lay hypnotist or hypnotherapist, for any hypnotist who has the opportunity of selecting (or rejecting) his prospective hypnotic subjects from a crowd can, by eliminatory tests, choose only those who are most responsive to his suggestions. In consequence of this he is more certain to be able to hypnotise his subjects. He naturally does not go looking for difficult subjects but begins to work on the most tractable and responsive, for success with his first subject is important and influences the others.

Many factors operated in favour of the entertainer hypnotist. The emotional expectancy and the anticipatory excitement of the audience did much to arouse their latent superstition which was helpful in creating the trance state in many of the subjects. In addition to this was the fact that the hynotist was a showman with all the polished patter of the professional.

Public Interest in Hypnosis

The public interest in hypnotism is comparatively recent, dating from approximately 1946-47, and from then until the Hypnotism Act in 1952 when hypnotic entertainments ended, many thousands of people throughout Britain must have witnessed hypnotic demonstrations. Though these demonstrations offended many of the sensitive who felt it an affront to human dignity to see adults running around on their hands and knees, growling like tigers or passionately hugging broomsticks, there were some positive gains resulting from these demonstrations. Witnessing them convinced many people that hypnosis was a fact which had been much doubted before these public demonstrations. It is significant that since that date hypnosis is slowly but surely being used as a form of medical treatment.

TERMINATING HYPNOTIC SESSION

Normally there will be no difficulty in waking a subject. The difficulty is to induce the trance, not to terminate it. To awaken the majority of subjects, the mere suggestion that they will open their eyes and be wide awake at a given cue (such as counting six, the word "six" serving as the cue) is all that is necessary to terminate the trance. This method will be successful with practically all subjects.

Arousing Subjects From Hypnotic State

It is a sound method, when instructing a subject, to tell him that you will count, but this time that you will count backwards, that you will count ten...nine... eight...and so on, and that when you arrive at the number "One" he will be wide awake, and that he will feel much better for having rested. Do not waken subjects too abruptly. It is better to err on the side of doing so too slowly, rather than too rapidly.

Arousing Deeply Hypnotised Subjects

If you are unable to wake a hypnotised subject, which is very unlikely, do not in any way be disturbed. See that he is resting comfortably and that he has no tight clothing, such as a necktie, to restrict his breathing. Then instruct him on these lines: "I am going to leave you to rest. In a short time you will find that you will become restless. You will not know why, but you will want to wake up. When you feel this restlessness you will start to count slowly to yourself, and you will find that when you get to nine and ten you will find yourself waking up. You will find that your eyelids begin to move as though they were going to open. By the time you get to fifteen "your eyes will open by themselves, and you will be wide awake." Then leave your subject and in all probability he will awaken after a short rest. If he does not do so, do not be at all disturbed but make arrangements so that he may be made comfortable either on a bed or a couch and give him the following instructions: "You will continue to rest and will shortly pass into a sound sleep, from which you will awaken, and feel refreshed." Do not let other people try to arouse him. The sleeper will awaken after a few minutes, or at most a few hours' sleep, and will do so whether the hypnotist is present or not.

No uneasiness should be entertained if a subject does not wake up immediately in response to your suggestions, for the trance state will of its own accord turn into ordinary sleep, from which your subject will wake in a perfectly normal manner. The length of time he will sleep will be dependent on how tired his body is. In this way hypnosis makes possible a degree of relaxation and recuperation which would not have been possible through his ordinary sleep.

Upon awakening from a hypnotic trance the subject undergoes a change in consciousness. This can be described as a regaining of will, of memory and of reasoning powers—a re-orientation or picking up of the threads of consciousness again. The time taken to awaken varies with different individuals.

After The Hypnotic Session

If any suggestions have been made to the hypnotised individual, the nature of which are antagonistic or contrary to his views, desires or interests, there is every probability of his harbouring a hostile feeling towards the hypnotist. He may be quite unconscious of this hostility, which may express itself in a variety of ways. He may, for example, be critical of the hypnotist or of his methods of procedure, and in consequence develop a mild resistance to the hypnotist's instructions to "wake up." If this occurs no uneasiness should be felt and the instructions given above should be followed.

Some people on awakening may express disappointment with the experience. They may insist that they had heard everything that went on, or that they were unaffected by the hypnotist. This arises out of misconceptions they entertain concerning the nature of hypnotism. The lack of consciousness and amnesia which they possibly anticipated is not experienced by some subjects until some hours have been spent in conditioning them. Nevertheless, though the individual may consciously believe that his trance was extremely light, or that he has not been hypnotically affected, the suggestions which have been made to him in most cases will exercise influence, that is unless the subject deliberately sets out very determinedly to prove that the suggestions will not work.

It will sometimes be the experience of the hypnotist that someone whom he has hypnotised will, on waking, insist that he has not been hypnotised. This attitude may be maintained even though it may be demonstrated to the subject that he cannot open his eyes. Even then some subjects will still insist that despite this evidence they could have opened their eyes, or stood up if they had wished. In these cases the character structure of the individual is such that he cannot admit that he has been dominated and was under the control of anyone else.

The majority of people who insist that they have only

experienced a light trance, should have the nature of the hypnotic trance explained to them, and should be told that it is perfectly normal that they should hear external noises and maintain rapport with the hypnotist.

Don't attempt to convince those who dogmatically maintain that they have not been hypnotised. Explanations will serve no useful purpose.

The popular idea of the hypnotised person remembering nothing on waking applies only to a few subjects. People's reactions differ. The majority remember most of what occurred when they are hypnotised, but in the main their recollections tend to be faulty. The fact must not be overlooked that our recollections in the waking state are likewise faulty. If, for example, a person is dozing, often he will indignantly deny the fact.

Some subjects, on awakening, can apparently remember everything that has occurred, but then the memories may fade in the manner a dream vanishes. Others on awakening may have no recollection, or a very hazy one, of what has occurred, but gradually detail comes back to them until they can recall everything that has happened.

Post-Hypnotic Suggestions of Amnesia

Suggestions made to the subject that he will forget everything that has occurred during the trance, may or may not be effective. The effectiveness of the inhibiting suggestion is determined by how it affects the subject's pride, sense of independence, interest, morals, conscience and general character structure, also the nature of the material to be repressed.

An amnesia whilst awake may be created in respect of the events occurring in a hypnotic trance, but in subsequent trances the events may be remembered.

In waking consciousness, after being hypnotised, the individual may often recall phrases or happenings which have occurred during the hypnotic trance, but he may attribute these phrases and incidents to the work of his own imagination, and be unaware that they are memory fragments of the trance. On the other hand, an hysterical subject is very likely to imagine during the hypnotic trance that incidents occurred which are purely products of his own imagination.

The Two Most Essential Rules in Hypnosis

On awakening a subject from the hypnotic state, the first question the hypnotist should ask himself is this: "Is the subject wide awake and thoroughly aroused from the hypnotic state?" He should reassure himself on this point and should, as an invariable rule, make certain that the subject is thoroughly wide awake, and that no trace of the hypnotic state remains, and also that there are no uncancelled post-hypnotic suggestions other than those designed for the subject's own good, such as being able to relax, etc.

Post-hypnotic suggestions are dealt with in the next chapter.

CHAPTER TWELVE

POST-HYPNOTIC SUGGESTIONS

Post-hypnotic suggestions are, in effect, "delayed-action" suggestions. They are the operating of hypnotic suggestions at a later date. For example, whilst a subject is hypnotised, suggestions may be made that when he is awakened he will perform some action at a given cue. The appointed time arrives and the subject, in a waking state and apparently fully possessed of his faculties, will carry out the appointed task. The suggestions need not be directed to the performance of a specific task, but to an attitude of mind. It may, for example, be suggested that the individual's attitude towards some fear will undergo a modification or change, and this—if there is no stronger counter-influence—will be so. Post-hypnotic suggestions, however, grow weaker with the passing of time. Therefore, they should be aimed at creating habits which enable the subject to adapt himself more satisfactorily to life. In this case they have every chance of being adopted in place of the previous faulty behaviour patterns. It is apparent that the mere repetition of general phrases such as: "You are feeling better," etc., have not the same value as suggestions which have been patiently and carefully prepared. Often to prepare these suggestions considerable time must be spent investigating the subject's symptoms and complaints, history, medical record, present environment with immediate obstacles and limitations, together with his whole attitude towards life.

Hypnotic Suggestions To Avoid

The suggestions which are made to a patient (for such he is if he is asking for assistance) must not only be things which he desires, but also those things which are capable of practical fulfilment—otherwise his condition will in no way be improved. It might be added in the framing of post-hypnotic suggestions definite instructions should be avoided which would directly alter the patient's life; that is to say, he should never be instructed to make a choice or a decision, i.e. change his employment, to marry, or to break off an association. A hypnotherapist who is consulted for aid is a technician being asked to make an adjustment in the mental and emotional life of the patient, so that the patient himself shall be able to live his own life confidently and with full volition and control, and to make his own decisions.

When a patient is being given palliative suggestions to allay anxiety, post-hypnotic suggestions are made in the following manner:

"In a few minutes I am going to wake you up, and when you awake you will find that a change has occurred. You will feel relieved and all traces of anxiety will have left you, and you will feel completely relaxed." This should be amplified at length on the lines of lessened tension and of physical and mental relaxation. The self-esteem and well-being of the subject must continually be kept in mind, and his confidence in, and assurance of the sympathetic attitude of the hypnotist must be maintained, otherwise suggestions made to him will have little real value. It is difficult to lay down hard and fast rules for administering hypnotic suggestions, as there are so many variable factors—the chief of which is the unconscious attitude of the patient.

Experimental Post-Hypnotic Suggestions

If, for experimental purposes, the hypnotist at any time tries out any experiments, he should see that there is no possibility of the subject "acting out" the "post-hypnotic suggestion" at a later date when he accidentally encounters the same cue. As for example, if the subject were told that when he saw a glass of water he would feel very hot, and the hypnotist forgets to remove this suggestion at the conclusion of the session, the subject might, some days later, be disturbed by a recurrence of the symptoms of increased temperature, induced by the sight of a glass of water. The hypnotist, therefore, having made any post-hypnotic suggestions, should as routine, take pains to cancel out all suggestions which are not designed for the well being of the subject.

It is wise to inform the subject later of the nature of suggestions which have been made to him whilst hypnotised. He may or may not remember them; if a deep state has been induced there may be amnesia, but this state is subject to change and he may later recall the suggestions. If, in these circumstances, he has not been fully informed by the hypnotist, the latter is likely to lose the subject's confidence.

Gaining Full Confidence of Subject

The object of the hypnotist is to gain the full and complete confidence of his subject. The suggestions made in the hypnotic state should be explained to the subject when he is awake, so that intellectually he is fully aware of the procedure of treatment. Consciously and subconsciously his motives are directed to, and should be working together for the same ends.

If post-hypnotic suggestions are made which would

create resistance on the part of the individual, he will become uneasy and make efforts to combat the impulse to perform any unwelcome suggestion. This tension and anxiety is, however, immediately resolved if the post-hypnotic suggestion is carried out. If the subject who has carried out a post-hypnotic suggestion is questioned as to why he has carried out the particular act, he will usually rationalise his actions and find the most ingenious explanations and excuses.

Persistence of Post-Hypnotic Suggestion

The effective duration of the post-hypnotic suggestion is to a very large extent determined by how it fits in with the character structure, tendencies and habits, of the individual, or how far it is in his interests. If post-hypnotic suggestions are in any way damaging or derogatory to his sense of self-esteem, they will tend to fade more rapidly than suggestions which would give pleasure or be profitable.

Post-hypnotic suggestions may, or may not, be recognised as such by the subject. He may, for example, (impelled by a post-hypnotic suggestion) have no idea why he has to rise and alter the hands of a clock, or to re-arrange the furniture. On the other hand, he may have a dim idea that he should do this, or even that it has been suggested to him during the hypnotic trance. In other words, post-hypnotic suggestions, like other hypnotic phenomena, produce varying reactions with different individuals.

CHAPTER THIRTEEN

SELF HYPNOSIS

One branch of hypnosis which has not received the attention it deserves is that of self hypnosis. As a result of using hypnosis in treating patients for over twenty years, it is my firm conviction that when instruction and coaching in self hypnosis is included as part of the hypnotic treatment, better and more permanent results are obtained.

There are, of course, exceptions when patients cannot be trusted to devise suggestions best suited to their needs and, in the case of these individuals, it is inadvisable to instruct them in these techniques.

Objects of Self Hypnosis

The main objective people have in mind when seeking hypnotic treatment is to cure some ailment, increase confidence or overcome some disability, in short, to gain more control over themselves . . . and certainly not to become robots, bereft of will power. As a result, for many people the idea of acquiring the ability to help oneself through self hypnosis has a strong appeal.

Whilst it is true that the hypnotherapist has sometimes to play the part of a "mental healer" when he cannot get his patient to co-operate by using self suggestion, he should, in my view, make every effort to explain the techniques of suggestion to his patient, and get him to carry out a daily session of self suggestion, for, in this way, the twin drawbacks of relapse and dependency on the hypnotist can be avoided. When the patient's aid is enlisted in this way his morale is strengthened by the fact that he is playing an active part in his own treatment, and he is also able to administer self suggestions on intimate or personal matters.

All Hypnosis is Self Hypnosis

It has been said that all hypnosis is basically self hypnosis, and there is much to support this view. It is the subject's belief and conviction that the hypnotist possesses the mysterious power to hypnotise people which in great measure invests him with this power. If the subject doubted the hypnotist's ability it is very unlikely he would be hypnotised.

Instruction and coaching patients in self hypnosis is greatly aided by the fact that when a trance has been attained, this "mysterious power" can be passed over to the patient by using post-hypnotic suggestions such as "You can do this yourself." As this opens up the very valuable auxiliary of self treatment, self hypnosis in my opinion is one of the most important branches of hypnosis.

Self Hypnosis in Africa and India

My belief in the value of self hypnosis was aroused many years ago as a result of my experiences when conducting hypnotic demonstrations during lecture tours, and in later years by witnessing the powerful effects produced by self suggestion when the impressionable imaginations and superstitions of various natives were influenced and manipulated by witch doctors and other indigenous medicine men and healers.

My belief in the power of self suggestion was further strengthened and confirmed by my own experience and training in Yoga in India, and again by the results achieved by members of classes whom I had instructed in the use of the techniques of self suggestion and self hypnosis, and lastly, by seeing daily the negative results of self suggestion in a wide variety of psychosomatic ailments and nervous troubles.

Example of Unconscious Self Hypnosis

One of the first examples of the power of self hynosis which I witnessed was in Sydney, Australia, many years ago. I was including a brief hypnotic demonstration in a lecture I was giving on psychology, and had called for some volunteers. Turning to one of the volunteers I made a motion of my hand for him to sit down. To my surprise he immediately went into a hypnotic trance. I had not spoken to him or tried in any way to hypnotise him. It was his own emotional expectation and mis-interpretation of my gesture which had caused him, unknowingly, to hypnotise himself. This volunteer was of the type in which the trance can be created immediately as described in earlier pages as the Instantaneous Method. The French psychologist, Janet, describes this type of hypnotic induction as instantaneous somnambulism, and it is an impressive example of self suggestion.

Again and again as I travelled in Australia, New Zealand, Africa and India, I found more and more corroboration of the power of self suggestion, not only in the results achieved and the changes made in their lives by members of the classes to whom I taught self hypnosis, but also in the lives of the followers of various religions and beliefs.

In Africa and India I took every opportunity of seeing indigenous healers, sadhus, witch doctors and medicine men, and all ceremonies concerned with healing sick people, and what I saw convinced me that suggestion and above all, self suggestion, was the all important factor in helping and healing those who sought their aid. Typical examples of self induced trances can be seen in the Indian religious ceremony of Kavady when the devotee renders his body insensitive to the pins which pierce his tongue and flesh. Somewhat similar ceremonies are to be seen amongst the Malays in the Khalifa where swords and fire are used during the ceremony. The African rituals are mainly concerned with dancing, drumming and chanting but in all these the repetitive drumming, dancing and chanting produce trances in many of those taking part.

Common Denominator Is Self Induced Trance

However dissimilar the above ceremonies might appear they have much in common, for most of the people taking part in them are seeking a cure for some sickness and the indigenous practitioner, whether he is a priest, medicine man or witch doctor, conducts a ceremony or ritual which is linked up with the tribal, religious or cultural beliefs and superstitions of the devotee or supplicant. These are the beliefs in which the follower or "patient" has been brought up, and he will conform and follow the ritual of dancing, chanting or whatever it may be, and after a while goes into a trance state (that is to say he has, in a greater or lesser degree, been hypnotised) and if he is a good subject and his complaint is psychosomatic, there is every probability of what in medical terminology is described as a spontaneous cure.

However bizarre the methods of these empiric practitioners might appear to Western eyes, they achieve about the same percentage of results as Western therapists, for psychosomatic ailments afflict the superstitious and the sophisticated alike.

Difference Is In Name Not Nature of Hypnotic State

Allowing for the more flamboyant procedures and colourful rituals, also for greater superstition and undeveloped critical faculty on the part of simpler people, the distinction between the creation of the trance state through native rituals and through clinical hypnosis is more a matter of terminology than any real or intrinsic difference.

From my own experiences in Yoga I came to the conclusion that the lower stages of the yogic trance are identical with what we in the West term self hypnosis. I think it is essential to keep in mind that no one school of psychology or any religious belief or philosophy, has a monopoly of the trance state which is a universal mental phenomenon observable in people of all races and of all levels of intelligence.

The trance, or self induced hypnotic state, can be achieved in a variety of ways, varying from religious ritual to a clinical hypnotic induction. It is also attributed to many different causes. Some people believe it is caused by the Gods, others by magic or spirits or just by self suggestion. It should be borne in mind that when attained, the trance state can be used to produce very different objectives, for instance insensibility to pain (analgesia), singlemindedness in study, a cure for some ailment, increased confidence, conducting research into Extra Sensory Perception or, as in Yoga, to develop spiritually.

The student hypnotist will find many advantages in learning all he can about self hypnosis, for in doing so he has the opportunity of playing the dual role of hypnotist and subject and also is able to make use of the techniques of self hypnosis and self suggestion in his own life.

CHAPTER FOURTEEN

INSTRUCTION IN SELF HYPNOSIS

The easiest way to help a good hypnotic subject to learn self hypnosis is to include in the induction a post-hypnotic suggestion such as "You will be able to hypnotise yourself." This is, of course, not all that is required, for it is also necessary to give some explanation and instruction on the lines which follow. It sounds very easy to give a simple post-hypnotic suggestion on the above lines, and then prescribe a simple ritual such as counting and including a phrase such as "and when you get to ten you will drift off into a hypnotic state and be able to make your own hypnotic suggestions to yourself," but it is not quite as easy as this, for a number of important points must be taken into consideration.

Protective Post-hypnotic Suggestions

As I have mentioned previously unless you consider the hypnotic subject is capable and realistic, and not likely to make foolish suggestions which could be harmful, it is inadvisable to teach him self hypnosis. Again, in the interests of those who are taught self hypnosis, a number of self protective suggestions can be included such as "If anyone should knock on the door, or enter the room in which you are carrying out a self suggestion session, you will become instantly wide awake and alert." Also when giving these protective post hypnotic suggestions to your subject you can include "If at any time, whilst you are in a self induced hypnotic state, you overhear any remarks, they will not influence you."

This later links up with a further suggestion of "only thoughts which are constructive and for your own good, will register in your unconscious mind." Another protective suggestion which can be included to prevent advantage being taken of the increased suggestibility created in your patient is, "No one will be able to hypnotise you unless you specifically ask for this to be done." If you should feel that an absolute veto is indicated, make the post-hypnotic suggestion. "No one will be able to hypnotise you unless you make the request in writing. If it is necessary for dental work or any other reason, you will write your request and give it to your doctor or hypnotherapist."

Another suggestion which is advisable with some people is to include something on the following lines, "You will never have any difficulty in waking yourself . . . if you do go into a deep hypnotic state it will turn into a normal sleep from which you will wake refreshed and in a perfectly normal manner".

Instructing Student In Self Hypnosis

When beginning instructions on methods of self hypnosis, if your subject or patient has no general acquaintance with psychological ideas, I would recommend that you start by giving him a general idea of how the unconscious mind controls and influences many of our bodily functions, moods and mental attitudes, and then explain to him how, through using self suggestion, this unconscious mind itself can be influenced.

Difference Between Talking To And TELLING People

The manner in which a hypnotist or hypnotherapist talks to his patient alters. One moment he is explaining or describing something and offering reasons, reassurances or proof of the soundness and the truth of what he says, in short, submitting what he says to the patient's critical faculty, and the next moment he is speaking in an authoritative fashion, with no intention or desire that what he says should be analysed or argued about.

Broadly speaking we could say when talking to people that we either submit what we are saying to their critical minds, or completely disregard the individual's attitude and TELL HIM. Very often in hypnotic treatment it is helpful to use this more emphatic or authoritative way of talking. This does not mean raising one's voice or being unduly emphatic, otherwise resistances or resentment might be aroused. When we explain anything to people they participate by thinking about what we say but when we *tell them* they play a purely passive role of acceptance.

When instructing in self hypnosis it is better to err on the side of being authoritative rather than too friendly and informal. Avoid smiling or making long pauses, for the hypnotist who smiles or is uneasy or hesitant makes his own work more difficult. The objective is, without arousing any resistance or resentment, to convey in your manner a firm authoritative attitude, and whilst being reassuring, not being too informal.

This more authoritative style of talking is determined not only by the tone of the voice but also by the choice of words, and in the following advice about instructing a patient in the hypnotic techniques, I have enclosed much of the text in quotation marks, to indicate that the remarks are intended as an indication of the way in which to talk to a subject, and are not addressed to the reader.

Text For Instructing Student

After making some introductory remarks about the unconscious mind and explaining how it can be influenced by hypnotic suggestion, I recommend beginning on the following lines: "You can help yourself a great deal by using self hypnosis. After I have explained more about self hypnosis, I will hypnotise you and make post-hypnotic suggestions to you that you will be able to hypnotise yourself. This will enable you to give yourself a hypnotic treatment every day if you wish to do so. Once you have mastered these techniques you will not need my help."

Describing The Hypnotic State

"When I hypnotise you, or you hypnotise yourself, you must not have the expectation of going off into some extraordinary mystical realm. It is simply a pleasant, relaxed experience. Actually you pass through this state twice every day without being aware of it . . . once when you wake up in the morning and again when you go to sleep. This transition from sleep to waking is not as sudden as it appears. Just as we drop off to sleep there is a rapid fading out of awareness, but briefly, just before we lose consciousness, we pass through what is called a hypnogogic state of consciousness. This is the borderland between the conscious and the unconscious mind, but our passage through this state is so brief that on awakening we have no memory of it.

"In the hypnotic and self induced hypnotic states normal consciousness is withdrawn and sinks, as it were, beneath the surface of your mind until it approaches the borderland or no-man's-land which divides your conscious from your unconscious mind . . . but, instead of sinking into oblivion, awareness remains poised midway between the conscious and the unconscious mind, and linked with both. It is because it is linked with both that it can relay instructions and suggestions to your unconscious mind.

"This relaying is carried out by letting your suggestions silently pass through your mind. In this state you are talking to yourself, and this is actually what is happening, for your conscious mind is talking to, or instructing your unconscious mind what to do. You could think of your conscious mind as the one who plans, like the manager of a business, and your unconscious mind as the workers. Sometimes the manager has to go down to the workshops himself and instruct the workers. In a similar way this is what you will be doing when you let yourself sink into a hypnotic state, and your awareness approaches the borderland of the unconscious mind and gives it orders.

Reassuring Your Subject

"Do not feel uneasy when I hypnotise you, or when you hypnotise yourself, for I will make suggestions which will safeguard you." If your subject shows any signs of being ill at ease, ask him if he has any misgivings or doubts. Say to him "Do not feel uneasy, no harm can come to you. When I hypnotise you I will make suggestions that you will relax and be at ease. Even without my suggestions part of your unconscious mind will remain alert like a sentinel, just as it does when you are asleep. If this awareness did not remain you would have no memory of dreaming, nor would you be awakened by any sudden noises. One part of your unconscious mind will be on duty to protect you whether you are hypnotised or asleep. You are asking your unconscious mind for its help and you must trust it to look after you. If you go into a deep trance when you hypnotise yourself it will turn into normal sleep."

Practical Arrangements

Make arrangements that the room in which you are conducting the hypnotic session is quiet, and that there is not likely to be any interruptions, also that the room is neither too hot nor too cold, and above all, that there are no draughts.

See that your subject is comfortably seated or lying down whilst you are making these introductory remarks. Tell him to relax whilst he is listening to you and, in this way, he will become more at ease, and more amenable to, and ready for your hypnotic induction.

No two hypnotists work alike for the simple reason that each one develops his own technique according to his personality and experience. An excellent way in which to commence an induction is to ask your subject to take a number of deep breaths. You can then begin to take control by saying "Now breathe in . . . deeper . . . deeper . . . that's right, now out . . . slowly . . . now in again." In this way, without any sudden take over, you can quietly assume an authoritative role and your induction will commence smoothly, easily and naturally.

Hypnotising Subject

Assuming that you are using a fixed gaze method of hypnotising, as instructed in an earlier chapter, hold some object—a ring or a pen will do—about eighteen inches in front of your subject's face, slightly above his eye level, so that he has to look slightly upwards. Then slowly move the object about six inches to the right, and then back to centre, then to the left. Move it slowly from side to side, telling your subject to keep his eyes fixed on it. Whilst you are doing this and his attention is focused on the object you are holding, continue talking and, in this fashion, you begin to create a split in his consciousness. Tell him that soon his eyes will begin to tire, and that involuntarily he will blink. When he does so tell him that his eyelids will begin to feel very heavy, and that it will become more and more of an effort for him to open his eyes. Keep on telling him this, varying your wording.

Soon his eyes will tire, partly because of the slight strain of the eyes being directed upwards, and partly because of the nearness of the object on which they are focused. You can, without the subject's knowledge, increase this strain whilst moving the object from side to side, by moving it slightly upwards and nearer to your subject's face. This increases the strain on the eye muscles.

The periods for which your subject's eyes will close will become longer. When this happens and you detect signs that his eyes are fatigued, tell him to rest with his eyes closed, and continue talking on the lines of the material given in earlier chapters for deepening the hypnotic state. To bring about this induction in which you are teaching self hypnosis you can use the above, or other methods of hypnotic induction described in Chapters Five and Six, but with practice you will soon begin to experiment with methods of your own.

Deepening Hypnotic State

Continue with your suggestions for deepening the hypnotic state until you judge from signs such as the head lolling over, or the body slumping or other obvious signs that your subject is hypnotised. If you are not sure continue with your suggestions, or you can make some tests, but it is best if you are uncertain whether your subject is hypnotised, to phrase your suggestions in such a way that he cannot disprove what you tell him. For example if you say "You cannot raise your arm" and he immediately raises his arm, which he may do if he is only lightly affected, your authority is weakened. If you are not certain it is more prudent to continue with the trance deepening suggestions for a longer period before making any positive tests. When you feel the subject is sufficiently relaxed begin to make the suggestions he has requested you to make, or make those which you judge would be helpful. When you have completed these, make the post-hypnotic suggestions that he will be able to induce this hypnotic state in himself and register suggestions in his own unconscious mind.

Post-hypnotic Suggestions For Self Hypnosis

It is better to give precise instructions on just how your subject is to carry out his self suggestion sessions. Prescribe a definite routine such as "When you are about to begin a self hypnotic session breathe deeply ten times, and as you do so you will begin to feel relaxed and sleepy. If you are lying down look at the ceiling, or if you are sitting, look straight ahead and count silently to yourself. When you get to 'ten' your eyes will close by themselves and you will then go on counting silently to yourself, getting sleepier and sleepier as you count. When you reach 'twenty' stop counting and rest, for you will have sunk down deeply enough to register suggestions in your unconscious mind."

Then remind him "When you reach this detached state, however light or deep it may be, this is when you let your suggestions float silently through your mind in the way I have already described to you."

Post-hypnotic Suggestions for Subject to Terminate a Self Hypnotic Session

Make post-hypnotic suggestions to your subject that he will never have any difficulty in waking himself from the hypnotic state. Prescribe some simple routine which he is to use to terminate his hypnotic sessions, such as counting backwards from "five" and that at "one" he will be alert and wide awake.

After you have concluded your hypnotic session with your subject and he is wide awake, check that he understands the routine of hypnotising himself, also of the way in which he is to rouse himself. It is also sound practice to have him go through the routine self induction in your presence, to make sure there are no points on which he is not clear. Impress on your subject that, even if he has been only lightly affected by hypnotic suggestions, the suggestions will "get through" to his unconscious mind. Even if subjects have been hypnotically affected only in a mild degree, the most surprising benefits from this self treatment very frequently come about.

Uses of Self Hypnosis

Self hypnosis has great value where a number of treatments are required, as in complaints of long standing, where time is necessary for the desired changes to come about, or in weight reducing or altering some habit, which might be as slow in going as it was in forming.

Self hypnosis is an invaluable method of treatment, for once the patient has been instructed and advised of the way in which he is to work, he can administer a hypnotic or a self suggestion session as often as desired, without the time and expense of visiting a hypnotherapist.

*Fully detailed techniques are described in *Self Hypnosis and Scientific Self Suggestion*, by W. J. Ousby.

CHAPTER FIFTEEN

HYPNOSIS AND HEALTH SERVICES

It is frequently stated by medical authorities, that a large proportion of illness today is caused by mental stress and emotional conflicts, and I have seen it estimated that approximately 60 per cent of our hospital beds are occupied by sufferers from this type of illness.

At the same time as illness of this type increases we are faced with the prospect of a critical shortage of doctors for some years to come. Implicit in the two above statements is the distressing fact that during the next few years an increasing number of sick people will, through lack of personnel, not receive the treatment they require. This unpleasant fact is, unfortunately, one of the many problems which must be faced in a rapidly developing society.

There is talk at the present time of a possible collapse of the National Health Service, but whether this happens or not, the unalterable fact remains that for some years to come there will be a shortage of doctors, and a steadily increasing number of sufferers from psychosomatic illness, and in considering this disturbing picture of the nation's health, it appears that a valuable means of aiding overworked doctors and of making therapy available to large numbers of people has not yet been fully recognised.

The views I am putting forward in this chapter are the results of over twenty years of therapeutic work. It is my experience that groups of people can be instructed in hypnotherapeutic techniques, and in this way learn to help themselves. If these methods were employed in the Health Services, particularly in the Preventive Health Service, they would bring about a short cut in psychotherapy comparable with some of the dramatic results achieved by antibiotics in the treatment of physical complaints.

The following proposals do not suggest that laymen should diagnose or give medical treatment, but that, working under the supervision of doctors, a register of approved hypnotherapists could give aid to many people who, because of lack of therapists, are unlikely to receive the psychological aid they require.

Hypnosis Is Not a "Cure All"

It is not for a moment suggested that hypnosis is a panacea for all illness, but, as many of today's ailments are caused by stress, worry and nervous tension, if those people who are likely at a later date to suffer illness on this account, could be instructed in relaxation and self suggestion techniques before their illness developed, much of today's psychosomatic ailments would be aborted or would never occur.

Prevention Is Better Than Cure

An expanded Preventive Health Service, incorporating group therapy using relaxation and self hypnotic and self suggestion techniques, could take much work off the shoulders of overworked doctors, who could send patients to groups where they could be instructed in relaxation techniques and coached in positive self suggestion.

Group Treatment in Self Hypnosis Could Provide a Short Cut

I know from personal experience that groups consisting of from ten to twenty people can be instructed in these techniques, and have conducted such groups in Australia, New Zealand, South Africa, Rhodesia, Kenya and Britain for a number of years. My experience is that most people dealing with stress, nervous tension and emotional problems require tuition in the personality skills of relaxation and self suggestion rather than treatment.

Despite all our scientific and technological advances, psychologically speaking, we are still in the "dark ages." We get an instruction book with a motor car or a sewing machine, but with ourselves, "the human machine," we get no such instructions.

Every human being will inevitably be faced with problems . . . problems of adolescence, of marriage, of parenthood, of middle age and of old age. If the individual is handicapped by some emotional trauma or other disability, these crises will exert greater strain. It is in the absence of such instruction that most psychosomatic illnesses develop, and yet they could be averted or absorbed by reassurance, relaxation instruction and tuition in self suggestion techniques.

In most cases a few hours instruction in relaxation, self suggestion or self hypnosis would prevent many people suffering years of misery, ill health and eventual breakdown, save doctors a great deal of time and the nation untold man hours.

Mass Hypnosis On Radio

Reverting to the practicality of such schemes, as far back as 1948 whilst on a lecture tour, I was invited by the New Zealand Government Radio Services to broadcast a programme to explain and coach listeners in some simple relaxation techniques, and also to carry out a mass hypnotic session over the radio, broadcasting suggestions of general relaxation and of general mental and physical welfare. This broadcast was well received as will be seen from the following letter from the New Zealand Broadcasting Services:

20th December, 1948

Dear Mr. Ousby,

As you were unable to check the results of your broadcast from Station 1 ZB before departing from New Zealand, I thought you would be interested to know how the listeners reacted.

The general tenor of coment in the mail received indicates that those who wrote enjoyed the relaxation brought about by your broadcast and thereby obtained beneficial results. As I indicated whilst you were here, I am sure that a series of treatments of this nature would bring about permanent relief to a lot of people.

We have not had one word of criticism or any unfavourable reaction of any kind to your programme, and I trust that when you return to New Zealand we will be able to broadcast a further series.

With best wishes,

Yours sincerely,

(signed) J. W. Griffiths
Station Manager, 1ZB

Auxiliary Medical Register of Hypnotherapists?

I am not for a moment suggesting that anyone but doctors should supervise this therapeutic work, but it would be to the benefit of all if a register of experienced hypnotherapists was formed and they were recruited into some Auxiliary Medical Register as a branch of the Preventive Health Service. I am sure that most hypnotherapists would, like myself, be willing to devote certain hours to such work on a voluntary basis in order to assist in the formation of such a scheme.

The advantages of hynotherapists being available at clinics where group therapy was being carried out would be that

(a) Doctors could send along tense and worried patients or those suffering from psychosomatic complaints to be taught how to relax and to be initiated in the self suggestion techniques so that they could help themselves by positive suggestions instead of unconsciously bringing about self induced illness.

(b) People who are at present unable to receive psychological aid because of shortage of therapists could receive reassurance through relaxation therapy pending psychiatric treatment.

(c) Further use could be made of such a register by hypnotherapists being attached to, or visiting hospitals to give hypnotic treatment to specified patients to prevent them from worrying and to help them to relax and to co-operate in treatment. Hypnotic suggestions would have very great value in reassuring those who have operations pending, and in helping in rehabilitation and in adjusting the mental attitudes of those who have to make terms with some permanent disability.

(d) Another very great service hypnosis could render would be to those who are fatally ill or about to die. Hypnotic suggestion could make their last hours easier. Their minds and bodies could be eased and courage and comfort given, particularly by therapists who themselves have strong beliefs in the meaning and purpose of life.

Hypnotherapy and the National Health Service

At the present time psychotherapy is the weak point in the nation's armoury in the fight against ill health ... for many illnesses are caused by mental and emotional stresses.

It is no dream to say that the hypnotherapeutic techniques (which in my view include relaxation, auto suggestion, self hypnosis and hetero hypnosis) could be a most powerful aid in strengthening this weak point in our medical services. This powerful aid is the healing force of Nature herself ... for just as broken bones will knit and torn flesh will heal, in the same way given the right conditions, nature will also soothe the nervous system, restore emotional equilibrium nad bring peace of mind.

Hypnosis is a natural healing agent which, correctly prescribed and administered, can, in a perfectly natural way, bring about a harmonious functioning of the mental, emotional and physical functions.

Sooner or later hypnosis will undoubtedly take its place in the National Health Service, and the sooner this happens the fewer will be the number of people who will suffer emotional distress and physical illness.

CHAPTER SIXTEEN

CONCLUSION

It is important that the student hypnotist should take his responsibilities seriously, and give very careful consideration to all the suggestions he will be making to his subjects.

The following are a number of points which should be kept in mind:

* Never attempt to hypnotise an unco-operative subject.

* Never hypnotise minors or children unless in the presence of parents or responsible witnesses.

* Obtain the permission or agreement of the husband, wife or parent of anyone who might be thought not to be a completely free agent.

* Get the subject's agreement, request or consent for the nature of the hypnotic suggestions which might affect his future life.

* At the end of each hypnotic session, see that your subject is fully awake and acting normally in every way before he leaves you.

* See that all the suggestions and post-hypnotic suggestions you have made to your subject during a session are cancelled, excepting, of course, those which are for his own good.

* Avoid use of the fixed-gaze methods with people whose eyes are weak, or who appear to be unusually nervous.

* Hypnotism is more easily induced in people who are expecting it to help them. There is an exception to this where the desire to receive help causes

over-eagerness or an anxious, nervous or tense condition.

* The first time an attempt is made to hypnotise a subject there may be a difficulty in inducing the trance. If the subject is not a good subject during the first induction, he may be only very lightly affected by your suggestions. On the second and third attempts the suggestions will have greater effect. Once any depth of trance has been effected, subsequent inductions become easier and easier. Post-hypnotic suggestions may be employed to deepen later trances, and facilitate the ease with which they may be induced. In the absence of any counter influences affecting the subject each successive trance becomes easier to induce.

* When you are carrying out experiments, tests, and attempting inductions, many unexpected incidents are likely to occur. If you are unprepared for them you may find yourself embarrassed or disconcerted. It is impossible to anticipate everything which is likely to happen. Therefore do not, in any way, be disconcerted. Preserve an appearance of perfect calm and self control, and maintain your prestige.

Policy and Suggestions on Giving Advice

A hypnotist may find that he is called upon to give advice upon a variety of subjects. These may cover illness, personal and domestic troubles, and occupational difficulties. So it is as well to have a set policy ready, and to observe it at all times. Make sure that anyone seeking advice on any matter affecting his health has seen his own doctor.

Do not give direct advice on major problems such as counselling a change of occupation or refusing an offer of other employment. In particular, avoid giving direct advice, or a decision, on domestic problems. Do not place yourself in a position whereby anyone later on may be enabled to say: "I did as you told me. Look what has happened. It's your fault!"

When you do express opinions, always give reasons for your views. It is wisest to explain all the factors of a case clearly, and to leave it to the subject to arrive at the right solution. Until the hypnotist is quite sure of the circumstances he is dealing with, he should avoid making specific suggestions.

Personal Beliefs

Care must be taken to ascertain the religious, social and political beliefs of a subject in order to avoid offending or making any suggestion incompatible with his beliefs, or injuring his susceptibilities.

Avoidance of Development of a Dependency

The hypnotist must avoid, at all costs, allowing the subject to unconsciously slip into the habit of considering the hypnotist indispensable to him. It is very easy, and often beneficial to the subject, to look upon the therapist as his guide, philosopher and friend, but it is undesirable that he should think that the hypnotist is indispensable to his daily living, and that he cannot get along without him. This, obviously, is inimical to the final objective, for the aim is to build up in the subject self-confidence and self-reliance. For this reason, the hypnotist must be on his guard against giving out too much help from the beginning of the contact, and this must be gradually decreased as progress is made.

Demonstration of Physical Feats of Strength

If subjected to excessive strain, bones can break and tissues can be injured whether a person is hypnotised or not. To avoid any possibility of injury do not attempt to cause a hypnotised subject to undertake unreasonable feats of strength. It is quite obvious that not only would such an occurrence be dangerous and distressing to the subject, but it would also be very damaging to the hypnotist. Carelessly or thoughtlessly planned experiments of this nature give much material for adverse criticism of hypnotism. In any experiments where some degree of muscular effort is required, enlist as your volunteers only strong young people.

Therapeutic Suggestions

If anyone should ask for hypnotic suggestions to remove pain, or to alleviate or cure an ailment, no hypnotist should ever do so without making further enquiries into the circumstances of the cause. Pain is usually nature's warning that something is wrong, and it would be wrong to block it out with hypnotic suggestions without enquiring further.

The hypnotist should, by asking the patient, discover how long the prospective subject has had his pain or symptoms, and what treatment he has received for it. From this information he will be in a better position to decide what he should do. For example, a headache might be nothing more than a temporary hangover from a late night, but, on the other hand, if it was recurrent or has been persistent it might possibly be the beginning of a brain tumour. A stomach-ache might be a temporary colic but, if the pain is severe, it could be an acute attack of appendicitis, and in the patient's own interest it would be better that he should see a doctor as soon as possible. If you decide to use hypnosis then suggestions should be made on the following lines, "Your pain will grow easier, but this will not make you cancel your intention to see your doctor. The relief from pain will last until you see your doctor but you must go and see him."

It is hardly necessary to point out that anyone intending to give therapeutic suggestions would be wise to become acquainted with the ground work of psychology and have a doctor whom, if necessary, could be approached for advice.

If a hypnotist is approached for help by some sufferer who has exhausted all possible orthodox methods of treatment without success, no objection can be taken to the hypnotist rendering what aid he can. He will find that in a number of cases he is able, if not to cure, to alleviate many complaints. If possible the hypnotist should attempt to get the unofficial blessing of the patient's own doctor.

* Hypnotism should not be regarded as a new means of living one's life or achieving objectives. It is a means to an end. The life of any individual should be lived, arranged and organised in full waking consciousness, and should be so constituted that he may live naturally and spontaneously. Hypnotism is only a means of building the habits necessary to live in a healthy, balanced manner. It is also a means of removing obstacles, habits and ideas which will interfere with this process.

* In learning to hypnotise people various difficulties and obstacles may arise to delay competence being achieved. Circumstances may interfere with the programme planned, opportunities for practice or suitable subjects may not be available. These set-

backs will adversely affect the beginner if he has not grasped the fact that he is also vulnerable to suggestion. If obstacles and delays occur—do not be discouraged. Once he encounters a good somnambulist, if he has followed the instructions with only moderate competence, he cannot fail to achieve a successful induction. Once this is accomplished his confidence will be established, and his failures forgotten. How soon he discovers his first somnambulist is simply a matter of luck—and perseverance.

PART TWO

FOREWORD by SIR PAUL DUKES, K.B.E.

Mr. Ousby's system will be of special interest to those who, while believing that hypnotism might well rid them of nervous troubles and wrong habits of living, would none the less hesitate to visit a hypnotist. If such people will persevere in carrying out the instructions given in these pages they will certainly be able to help themselves in ways of which they have never dreamed. During recent years, both in Britain and America, soldiers have been trained by using self hypnotic techniques to render themselves immune from pain and even to undergo torture without betraying military secrets. The self-hypnotic trance is undoubtedly the secret which enables firewalkers and fakirs to perform their feats.

Mr. Ousby's presentation of the subject is eminently practical for use in everyday life. He is a scientific hypnotist skilled in the Eastern and Western techniques and by profession a psychoanalyst. His aim is to show the essentially simple yet powerful working of the mind under suggestion, and the methods whereby its technique can be systematically applied to oneself while retaining full volitional control.

The key to success lies in the ability to implant suggestions in the unconscious mind. With this in view the author has set forth a method of progressive physical relaxation through which control is gradually extended to mental and emotional mastery. The reader is shown how he is, in his present condition, actually hypnotising himself by his doubts and fears, and he learns how to reverse the process so that his subconscious mind diverts the elemental energy of his thoughts into constructive channels. Not the least merit of this Course is its profound sincerity. There is no doubt that the author is imbued with a deep desire to help all who are willing to make the initial effort to help themselves.

(signed) PAUL DUKES

INTRODUCTION

Broadly speaking there are four groups of people who are aware of the tremendous power suggestion possesses to alter people's lives.

Firstly the politicians, advertising and public relations specialists who influence public opinion.

Secondly the individuals who have learned the subtle art of using this powerful force upon themselves through the self suggestion or auto hypnotic techniques.

Thirdly those whose work is to treat with, and teach others how to use these techniques for gaining greater mental and emotional control and overcoming psychosomatic ailments.

Lastly those who have come to realise they need assistance in freeing themselves from the influence of negative thought, worry or some psychosomatic ailment which defies all effort of will and logic to displace it.

It is my conviction that an individual who has had a nervous breakdown and dealt with it successfully is far better equipped to face life than someone who has never been through this experience. This is because in this critical battle for self control, inner strengths and resources are revealed which otherwise would never have been discovered.

There is a story of ancient India which in allegorical form tells us something of the mysterious Unknown, or equally mysterious unconscious mind from which our

mental and emotional life springs ... and how in acquiring knowledge of the latent strengths and potentialities we
all possess, we are also acquiring superior weapons for
dealing with the problems we all have to face in life.

The story tells how Prince Arjuna, about to fight a
critical battle, decides to go to the mountains to ask the
God, Siva for superior or secret weapons with which to
win this battle. On the way in a forest clearing he sees a
deer which he shoots for food, but at the moment he shoots
a stranger steps from the trees and also shoots the deer.

Arjuna, who by nature was proud and headstrong,
angrily called out "You have no right to shoot the deer. I
saw it first and it is mine." The stranger replied "You are
foolish to think you can settle disputes by fighting, and if
you are as bold as you are foolish I must teach you a
lesson." Arjuna's pride would not let him take back his
arrogant words, and he could not avoid the challenge. So
raising his bow he loosed an arrow at his opponent. To his
amazement the stranger brushed his arrows aside. When
Arjuna had fired all his arrows, he drew his sword but the
stranger instantly disarmed him and held him in an iron
grip like a helpless child. Disarmed and unable to move
Arjuna closed his eyes and humility took the place of
arrogance and with passionate sincerity he prayed to the
Gods to save him from his helpless plight.

As soon as Arjuna prayed for help he found himself free
and unharmed and saw his adversary was Siva who had
manifested himself in human form as the embodiment
of the human spirit.

In the story, Siva says, "I wanted to help you but you
would not listen. You thought you could do everything
unaided. Did you think the powers which created you had
abandoned you? I wanted to give you superior weapons

but you would not listen or ask me until I made you helpless."

Arjuna then realised that he was not a lonely figure battling against the Unknown but that forces stronger than himself could be called on to help him in his critical battle.

We, like Arjuna, by resolving our inner conflicts can free energy and unsuspected inner resources and so accelerate recuperative and healing powers; in short turn the unconscious mind into a powerful ally which will aid us in living a healthier and happier life.

CHAPTER ONE

THE UNCONSCIOUS MIND

The following pages describe a simple "do it yourself" method of making alterations in oneself which cannot be achieved by will power alone. It goes beyond the simple reiterative principles of Coueism or any short-term methods of boosting will power.

These methods are successfully used to cure, prevent or alleviate a wide variety of complaints, but their application is not restricted to the remedial. They are being adopted as part of the personal techniques of many business and professional men and women, so that they may achieve greater efficiency with less wear and tear on the human machine.

A knowledge of natural laws is giving contemporary man ever increasing ability to harness and control electronic and atomic energy; in a similar way an extension of his knowledge of laws governing mental and emotional energies, gives him increased control over his own mental and emotional life. In the following pages it is shown how nervous energy can be diverted into constructive channels, instead of being fuzed off in damaging tensions or negative thoughts and emotions.

Most of us have witnessed the efforts of young children trying to write, faces screwed up, heads craned forward, shoulders hunched, tension in every limb and feature. During these ill co-ordinated efforts to make a few lines on paper with a pencil, about one hundred times the necessary energy is being employed. People suffering from nervous tension resemble these small children, but, unlike them, many will not correct their mistakes, and later, through not knowing how to relax inner tensions, ruin their health through well meant but wrongfully directed efforts.

Those who have acquired their own personal techniques of relaxing and using self suggestion or auto hypnosis, usually accomplish much more work than ordinary people, and in times of crisis or difficult circumstances can act with a cool, calm detachment. Sir Winston Churchill was an excellent example of mental control and personal technique. His competent handling of men and events arose out of his ability to maintain his own mental clarity, energy and zest for work, which in turn arose out of his ability to relax at will.

Sir Winston once asked if a certain man had the ability to relax and, on hearing that he had not, remarked "He will not last." This comment could be made of many business men. Nervous strain is inseparable from positions of responsibility today, and stress complaints are now occupational risks of those in executive positions.

Those people who had tremendous capacity for work and leadership—Caesar, Napoleon, Leonardo da Vinci, Gandhi, Michael Angelo, Schweitzer, Nuffield, Nelson, Churchill and numerous others did not rely on "driving" themselves, but had developed more informed methods of achieving peak performances of any tasks they undertook. The list of their qualities is almost identical—they had unfailing confidence in themselves, unusual powers of mental concentration, retentive memories, the ability to influence others, unusual capacities for work and the ability to sleep for short periods whenever they chose to do so.

It might be thought that these men were fortunate and that they had been endowed with outstanding qualities at birth, but in most cases this was not so—these qualities were discovered during periods of adversity.

They discovered

(a) That the average man uses only a fraction of his real potential

(b) That they could make greater use of their own latent abilities

(c) That this could be achieved without plundering their reserves of energy.

Sometimes the handbook of a motor car contains a simple explanation of how the engine works. The simplest explanation of how "the human machine" operates is to assume that man has two minds, a conscious mind and an unconscious mind. These two minds are separated by some form of barrier or curtain. The conscious mind does the thinking and "willing" and behind the curtain which separates these two minds the unconscious mind, working quietly in the background, regulates the major part of the activities necessary for living. It transforms food and oxygen into tissues and energy. It regulates the routine functions, co-ordinating the activities of all the organs of the body, the heart, stomach, liver, lungs, etc. It superintends the maintenance and repairs which the body requires—broken bones will knit, torn flesh will heal, antitoxins will be manufactured to combat fevers and in addition to this, the unconscious mind also controls almost all the functions of the physical and emotional life—it has absolute power over the routine functions. Nature, it has been said, would not trust man to digest his food by his own efforts, because through his carelessness or forgetfulness he would soon starve to death. The unconscious mind, with robot like efficiency, controls all the organic functions of the body and consciously man is unaware of all this complex inner activity. This arrangement leaves the conscious mind free to attend to activities in the outside world ... and the arrangement works very satisfactorily if nothing happens to upset the automatic activity of the unconscious mind.

Nervous tension is the most common cause of interference with what should be the smoothly co-ordinated operations of the unconscious mind.

The first intimation a man has that something is wrong may be a mild attack of indigestion, or he feels nervy and cannot relax, or maybe is not sleeping well. He may become aware that the robot unconscious mind is keeping tensions switched on and that he cannot get instructions through to it to switch off. This is the condition loosely described as nervous tension, and is the basic cause of most stress complaints.

Animals possess a much simpler nervous system and lead a less complicated life than we humans. Because of this we can see, by observing them in the wild state, what happens under stress. In Kenya I once saw a herd of zebra grazing quietly. Suddenly a lioness, which had crept near them under the cover of some undergrowth, made a charge, but immediately she appeared in the open the whole herd galloped off. The lioness, failing to get within striking distance, soon gave up the chase. The zebra gradually slackened their pace and, as the lioness stopped, although they had only moved a short distance, they also stopped, and to my surprise began grazing again as though nothing had happened. It will illustrate how the physical and nervous system operates if we examine what happened to the zebra during this alarm.

Immediately an alarm is given chemical and physical changes in the body take place at lightning speed. Sugar from the liver, together with secretions from the adrenal glands, is released into the blood stream, blood pressure rises, and the animal is poised, senses alerted, muscles tensed, ready for instant action either to take refuge in flight or to stand and fight . . . all other body processes (such as digestion) which are not essential to deal with the emergency, are suspended. When the danger has passed all tensions subside, digestive processes are resumed and all activities go back to normal.

Man has a much more complicated nervous system than the zebra, and because of this and the demands of life today his tensions do not switch off as easily as those of an animal. As a result few people are immune from nervous tension, and the prevalence of these tensions can be gathered from the frequent statements by medical authorities that the major part of all illness is caused by unsolved and emotional problems . . . that is by nervous tension.

With many people today the unconscious mind is in a semi-permanent state of alert, creating a wide variety of psychosomatic and nervous complaints, but it can be influenced to switch off unnecessary tensions and so allow the body's natural recuperative powers to restore the rhythm of physical, mental and emotional functioning and also, at the same time, to allow constructive self suggestions to be implanted in the unconscious mind to deal with specific and individual problems. The potential scope and value of the hypnotic, auto hypnotic and self suggestion techniques in helping others and oneself, is only fully realised by those who have some experience of these techniques.

The famous scientist J. B. S. Haldane gives some indication of the promise these techniques have for mankind in the following comment, "Anyone who has seen even a single example of the power of hypnotism and suggestion must realise that the face of the world and the possibilities of existence will be totally altered when we can control their effects and standardise their applications as has been possible, for example, with drugs which were once regarded as equally magical."

The hypnotic and modern suggestion techniques are in the same position today as penicillin and other antibiotics were a generation ago. At that time many people desperately needed the help that these precious drugs could have given them, but not sufficient was known of their large scale manufacture to make them freely available. The self hypnotic and self suggestion techniques taught in the following pages have been a turning point in the lives of many people, not only in curing ailments but in overcoming the problems of everyday life.

CHAPTER TWO

"GETTING THROUGH" TO THE UNCONSCIOUS MIND

This Section contains further comments about the unconscious mind and begins instructions on the first steps in making contact with it.

The average individual has many demands made on him. During the whole of his waking hours his eyes and ears are kept busy with a succession of sights and sounds, and, at the same time, a ceaseless stream of thoughts flows through his mind, as often as not accompanied by emotional activity.

Much of this activity is carried out by the unconscious mind, but frequently much more energy and effort than should be necessary is taken up in performing these activities. By giving a little attention to the way in which the unconscious mind can be influenced vast improvements can be made in the way it performs any task.

Although not aware of it everyone, by means of the unconscious mind, already performs extraordinarily complex activities. For example, a man walking down a busy street is thinking of some problem. There will be all the sights and sounds which go to make up the noise and distraction of a street. The man, busy with his own thoughts will pay no attention to the noise or the shop windows or people passing, but should a friend come walking towards him, or should someone suddenly call his name, his thoughts will be instantly switched to his friend or to the person who has called out his name. Although he was not consciously aware of all the sights and sounds going on around him, his unconscious mind had been busy noting them all . . . but like a good servant had not reported to him matters which were of no importance, in this way leaving his conscious mind free to attend to more important matters, while his unconscious mind attends to routine matters. In short, the unconscious mind of any reader, though he may never have thought about psychology, is already highly trained, and if he wishes, he can delegate to it many tasks which it can carry out much more efficiently than can be done by use of the conscious mind.

The success of all suggestion depends on gaining co-operation of the unconscious mind . . . and if it is approached with sincerity and patience it will allow man to tap energies he never dreamed he possessed, carry out feats which seemed impossible and cure complaints which had been regarded as hopeless, but this is dependent on his working *with*, and not *against* the laws which govern our being.

Whatever task faces one in life, whether it is to cure an illness, alter a habit or make a success of a job, or master the techniques of self suggestion there is no more important question than "How can I get the co-operation of my unconscious mind?"

Often when trying to influence his unconscious mind a man may encounter obstacles. Sometimes when he exerts his will to influence his unconscious, he may discover there is in the structure of the mind, something which prevents his instruction "getting through." He may say to himself "I am not going to smoke another cigarette" but later finds he is still smoking, for some reason his instructions have failed to get through to his unconscious mind.

The man trying only with his will power and courage

to overcome his problem may think it is a defeat to admit he cannot force his unconscious mind to do what he WILLS—but he can, like Arjuna, acquire the superior weapons which will enable him to succeed.

We cannot force our unconscious to work for us, but we can get its aid by using more informed methods. These methods enable us to enlist the help of the positive elements in the unconscious mind which are themselves striving to restore harmonious functioning.

The task of getting suggestions through to the positive elements in the unconscious mind is simplified, if we think of our mental make up as a business house with departments on different floors. On the first floor are the joint managers, the Intellect and the Will, these represent the conscious mind. On the lower floors are the workers who will carry out any orders they are given, and whose work it is to maintain the routine functioning of the emotional and physical life. These workers broadly speaking represent the unconscious mind. They are protected by a guard whose function is to prevent orders getting through to these workers, for they will do what they are told irrespective of what it is or who tells them. The guard is there to stop them, otherwise people after watching a TV programme would rush out and buy detergents, foods or anything else the scientifically designed suggestions of the TV advertising had instructed them to purchase.

Continuing this simplified picture of getting suggestions through to the workers in the unconscious mind, we first adopt the strategy of lulling the guard into a quiescent state and quietly passing messages to the helpful workers, who are themselves striving to correct whatever deviation there may be from a healthy happy life. The first step in lulling the guard is achieved by carrying out physical relaxation.

Though relaxing sounds simple, it is something which has to be learned and there is no one who cannot learn to relax, however tense he may be if he is patient and persistent. Once the ability is acquired it is as though shutters have been drawn on the outside world and attention is turned inwards. Recuperative processes begin and energy replenishes tired muscles, energy levels rise, and the guard is lulled into a quiescent state, creating favourable conditions for administering self suggestions.

The following instructions deal with General Relaxation which is a helpful condition for the creation of self hypnosis or the state of maximum suggestibility. The object in view is to attain a physical state in which tension is absent. This state is brought about not by learning new things to do, but by stopping various activities which are already going on.

Some people will find that if they spend a minute or two in deep breathing before the relaxation session it helps them to unwind and to "let go" more rapidly. This does not apply to everyone and by experiment you will see if it is helpful or otherwise to you personally.

The following exercises deal with the cultivation of relaxation, or "letting go" by cultivating muscular limpness. When the body is relaxed, mental and emotional activities, are influenced by this physical relaxation and are also quietened down. These are the first steps in "letting go."

When a limb is relaxed it is limp. It will lie motionless and inert. If it were lifted, bent or moved by someone else, no resistance or rigidity would be detected. It will move easily as though it were a piece of limp rope.

This relaxation is employed naturally by many animals, of which the cat is a good example. The flaccid way in which it can let its muscles relax completely, is very instructive and helpful by way of illustration in carrying out the following exercises.

In speaking of relaxation, the term "letting go" has been used. The question might be asked: "Letting go of what?" The answer would be to let go the tensions which cause restlessness and lack of ease. The difficulty with many people is that they have become habitually tensed up, and this overactive state of their nerves has become their normal condition. They have forgotten how to "let go."

To achieve relaxation it is necessary to let the tensions die down—but, as we have said, the tense individual may not be fully aware of all the tensions in himself. Some of the signs are to be seen in frowns, blinking, restless movements, and a lack of repose. The first exercise is directed towards educating the individual to recognise tension in himself as the first step to removing it. When he can recognise its presence he can also recognise its absence. Relaxation is nothing more than the absence of tension.

If, during the first attempts, when carrying out the exercises your attention is distracted by some imaginary stiffness, or awkwardness in posture, or involuntary swallowing, and the like, do not attempt to force these distractions out of your mind. They cannot be banished by a direct effort of the will. As far as possible turn the whole of your attention to the detail of the particular exercise upon which you are engaged. You may fail a number of times, but if you persevere repeatedly, the distractions will gradually cease as the nervous activity, of which the irritations are merely symptoms, quietens down.

The messages which may be flashed into consciousness such as: "My neck is stiff," "My mouth is dry," and so on, are due to the overactive sensory nerves. The fidgeting, twitching and other movements are due to motor nerve impulses, which are consciously or unconsciously attempting to relieve the real or imagined irritation. Tension in some degree is always present, even when we think we are relaxed. Our purpose is to reduce this tension to a minimum so that the symptoms of this overactivity cease.

CHAPTER THREE

GENERAL RELAXATION

This section gives you basic instructions on physically relaxing, and using self suggestions to increase your powers of positive self suggestibility and the creating of a trance state in subsequent sessions. At this stage some beginners may feel doubtful about their powers of self suggestibility, these doubts are not unnatural considering they have failed to use positive self suggestion but these doubts vanish, as the Course proceeds. It is not that people lack the power to suggest to themselves . . . as is all too evident in the results of damaging self suggestion. What they lack is the knowledge of how to *positively* employ this power of self suggestion.

This General Relaxation Exercise may take some time and have to be repeated for a number of sessions, but later the trance state, or a vastly increased state of suggestibility can be created fairly quickly without the routine of relaxing. Every time you carry out these preliminary exercises you will benefit if you will incorporate the prescribed suggestions which are to be used at the termination of each session.

To begin your General Relaxation Sessions isolate yourself where you will not be disturbed. If there is a possibility of this, lock your door.

It is best to choose a time when there is as little noise as possible. If there are, or are likely to be, outside noises, use cotton wool or ear plugs to deaden these sounds. It is wise to choose a time when you are not too tired or worried, and there are no tasks requiring your attention immediately after your exercise session. In short, arrange matters, as far as possible, so that you have a free mind. To this end it will be found helpful if you can arrange to be quiet for an hour or so preceding the first sessions. After you have carried out the exercises several times, it will be found that these preliminary preparations are no longer required.

Make yourself comfortable on a couch or a bed with, or without a pillow, as suits you best. Some people find that they can relax better on the floor with a carpet or a rug to lie on, but the reader after experimenting, will be the best judge of what suits his own needs. A small flat cushion or pad may also be found helpful, either in the small of the back or behind the knees. Spend a little time experimenting until the best conditions conducive to relaxation have been arranged.

When you are satisfied from your experiments that you have found the best conditions in which to be as comfortable as possible, lie on your back with your hands open and arms by your sides, but do not let them touch your body. Just let them rest comfortably at your sides, rest quietly and easily, looking at the ceiling. Don't stare but concentrate your gaze on one spot. Don't try to do anything else. Close your eyes if it is an effort to keep them open, but do not try to "put yourself off." The object of this resting is to let your mind and body gradually slow down. If your mind starts off on some task of its own, such as making out a shopping list, or working on some problem, bring it back and remind yourself of what you are doing. After a brief interval, particularly if you have been busy previously, you will feel various tirednesses of which you were not conscious before. You will be able to feel these sensations of tiredness specifically located in various muscles in the arms, legs, hands, back, shoulders and feet.

The next step is to mentally "feel" each of these in turn.

Let yourself relax as far as you can. Then direct your attention to your right hand and let it remain there for about ten seconds, then transfer your attention to your left hand, and then to your right foot, and then to your left foot, again spending about ten seconds on each. After this transfer your awareness to the sensations present in the muscles of the face, lips, tongue and mouth. As far as possible avoid moving any of these parts.

You will find that when you direct your attention to one part of your body you will forget all the other parts of your body. Go over your hands, feet and muscles in your face, as just directed three times. You will notice as the exercise proceeds, that any tensions which may have been present when you commenced the exercise will begin to ease and die down.

A verbal description of the process of acquiring a new sensory perception must, of necessity, be inadequate. The first part of the exercise which we are now describing is directed towards recognising this feeling of tension, and becoming aware of its varying degree of strength—or, what is the same thing, to recognising the absence of tension which is, of course, the state of being relaxed.

Even if you think that your progress is excellent, devote at least three sessions to the above exercise before attempting to proceed further, now experiment by directing your attention to different parts of your body. Progress is being made when it is found that the attention can be directed over the biceps, the muscles of the forearm, wrists, thighs, calves, ankles, feet, shoulders, back, neck and facial muscles without the mind wandering away from the task for a moment. It will be noticed after several sessions that an increasingly pleasant feeling of ease and comfort is experienced after this routine of General Relaxation. Also it will be found that restlessness has disappeared, and it is possible to stay resting immobile for longer periods without any movement.

To some, this exercise may constitute the greatest hurdle, and everything else that follows may, by comparison, seem easy. One test of having made progress is a growing awareness of the very different and distinct characters of the two sensations of relaxation and tension. A second way in which progress can be gauged is the manner in which it is possible to direct attention to the awareness of any part of the body, for example, an arm, and forget everything else.

The practice sessions should last at least five minutes and preferably should be carried out at least once a day, the longer the sessions and the more frequently they are carried out the better. The quality or standard of the general relaxation achieved will continue to improve with practice, as the effects of the work are cumulative. There is no one particular time which is best, many people find a session just before retiring produces very good results.

When you have attained some degree of familiarity with your relaxation exercises and they can be carried out more or less automatically, you are ready to take the first real step in using the self suggestion techniques. This is by beginning to carry out daily self suggestion sessions.

To revert to our example of the mind resembling a business house in which the managers, that is the Will and Intellect (the conscious mind) are sometimes prevented from getting messages through to the workers in the unconscious mind by a guard who acts as a kind of censor. This is the reason for the relaxing exercises as a result of which the guard can be lulled into a quiescent state, and so enable the managers to quietly pass on their messages in the form of suggestions, to the workers who are the positive elements in the unconscious mind.

Each one of us has his own pace in learning these techniques. There are very few people who can master this General Relaxation routine immediately. The average individual finds the first exercise needs a fair amount of repetition, but if he begins to make the suggestions recommended he will receive benefit. Do not try to go ahead too quickly as this could defeat its own purpose, for if we try to rush matters or use force we wake up the guardian who may stop our suggestions getting through. In other words, the more relaxed you are the more easily will your suggestions get through to the unconscious mind.

As a general principle the simpler the suggestions are the better. Concentrate on making suggestions of gradual improvement. When you are relaxed mentally repeat to yourself the suggestions recommended at the end of the paragraph. You can alter the actual wording of the suggestions as long as the meaning is unaltered, but it is advisable to have the patience to limit yourself to the general meaning of these suggestions. They serve as a foundation, once you have learned the techniques you can make all manner of suggestions but first make sure of establishing some foundation on which to build.

"I am going to have the patience to learn this technique and mobilise all the positive elements in my make-up and get rid of my problems and troubles."

"I am going to master this technique of suggestion."

"I am going to get my unconscious mind to work for me and not against me."

DIFFERENTIAL RELAXATION

When you are satisfied that a fair standard of General Relaxation has been achieved, you are ready to deliberately create local muscular tensions, so that they may be more closely examined.

Exercise No. 1

This exercise is carried out as follows:—Whilst lying relaxed, without in any way altering the position of your body raise the right arm until, with fingers straight out, the arm is raised about six inches off the couch or floor on which you are lying. See that it is extended stiff and straight, whilst the left arm remains limp by your side. Pay particular attention to seeing that no other movements of your body, limbs or features have been made, and that, apart from the muscles involved in raising your arm, you are completely relaxed. Whilst the arm is extended, mentally note the different sensation of tension in this arm from that in the rest of the body. Switch your attention to the tense arm and then to the limp one and contrast the sensation in each.

When the character of the relaxed state of your body, as different from the tenseness of your arm, is quite plainly felt, start to increase this difference in sensation by intensifying the tension in the right arm by tensing the muscles. Keep them tense for about two to five seconds, but when this becomes slightly painful let the arm go limp and drop.

Let it rest until the sensations of tension or tiredness disappear and the feeling is replaced gradually by the pleasant feeling which comes when tension or strain is absent. Note the sensations not only in a general way, but also as they are specifically located in the fingers, the hand, forearms, in the bicep and the shoulder muscles. Repeat the exercise with the left arm whilst resting the right arm. When the different character of the sensation of relaxation and tension has consciously been identified in both arms, repeat the exercise but this time do not lift the arm. The arm should now be left lying at your side, but the muscles are to be tensed so that the feelings of tension are experienced. Then "let go" the tension and wait until the pleasant feeling of relaxation is felt. This may take some minutes. Again tense the muscles, but this time do not tense them so strongly, or for so long. Rest again until the feeling is one of relaxation, and continue to rest and feel this relaxation becoming more complete. Reinforce your efforts to relax now by using mental suggestion. Whilst mentally making suggestions, watch that you do not unconsciously start to move your lips and tongue as though you were speaking. The suggestions are to be made mentally only.

The sequence should be:

(1) Tense the muscles
(2) "Let go"
(3) Rest
(4) Note the sensations
(5) Whilst resting, use suggestions to "let go" a little more each time. The suggestions to be employed are, "My arm is becoming more relaxed," "My arm is feeling more and more relaxed each time I do this exercise." Repeat these suggestions a number of

times. Continue with suggestions which seem most helpful and most conducive to "letting go" or decreasing tension.

Remember, when we think we have relaxed to the utmost, we have not really done so. When we rest, use suggestion and our tensions will subside of their own accord, providing we do not rush matters or try to get results too rapidly.

Exercise No. 2

For this exercise, lie down, relax and when completely at ease, stretch out the right leg and stiffen it. The toe should be pointed down, as though you were trying to touch something with your foot, just beyond your reach. Do not lift your leg, just stretch it, whilst letting its weight be supported by whatever you are lying on. Hold this position, until you can locate tensions separately in your thigh, calf, ankle and foot muscles. As soon as you locate them, relax and let your leg settle down under its own weight, and mentally note the difference in sensations in exactly the same way as in the previous exercise with your arms. This comparison, is, of course, purely a mental comparison. When you have rested for a short period, again tense the left leg, but this time the tension must be a little less and for a shorter period. Again rest, and notice the difference in sensations.

Exercise No. 3

For this exercise lie down and relax, then tighten or tense the muscles in the small of the back so that it is slightly arched. Hold this tension for a few seconds, and then draw in the abdominal muscles so that the stomach is pulled inwards and upwards. Hold this for a few seconds, and then relax. During the tension period the lower part of the back will be lifted clear of the support on which you are lying. Do not use a great deal of effort, no more than is necessary to raise your back about one inch. Then relax.

After this exercise has been carried out three times the exercise of the trunk is varied by shrugging the shoulders, and after holding them hunched up for a few seconds, letting them flop relaxed. It will be found that through the attention being first directed to one group of muscles and then to another, it is possible by this means to achieve a greater degree of relaxation than was possible before you identified these groups of muscles separately. During this exercise concentrate on the idea that all the muscles of the trunk are limp and that none are tense or taut.

Exercise No. 4

Each successive exercise adds further groups of muscles to those already relaxed. In this way relaxation already achieved becomes more complete.

When relaxed, gently let the head roll from one side to the other. Do this very slowly, letting it fall under its own weight from right to left. When the head has turned over as far as it will go in one direction, let it stay there for a while. Feel the heaviness of the facial flesh as it tends to sag. Your jaw muscles should not be clamped, but relaxed, and as a result your mouth may open slightly. Relax your tongue, which will lie flaccid in your mouth. When you have located the various sensations or sensory perceptions in your face, lips, tongue, etc, roll your head slowly over to the other side, and again note the sensations. In the periods of rest during this exercise, which should be performed very slowly, you may feel a degree of mental detachment greater than you have encountered so far.

Concentrate on relaxing the head, neck and facial muscles and aid this process by continued suggestions of relaxation.

The object of the preceding exercises is to acquire a new sensory perception. This is not easy in the beginning because the feelings or sensations are vague, indistinct and some are not in clearly defined areas, until some practice has been carried out. The sensations become clearer and more definite with continued practice. The general attitude of mind in performing the exercises should be to take it easy, with no attempt to hurry or rush. They are to be performed physically in an easy going, languid manner, but mentally remaining fully attentive. In the tensing movements use very little effort, the less the better. The object of the exercises is not physical exercise, but the reverse.

It will be clear that the relaxation exercises are a means of quietening and slowing down the mental and emotional activities so that messages can be passed quietly into the unconscious mind.

When we relax and shut our eyes we tend to drift towards a sleep or trance state, that is if we do not keep the mind switched on. Do not think you must go into a deep trance to get suggestions through to your unconscious mind. This is not so. Your suggestions will get through even if you have attained only the lightest of trances. It is true that you may have to patiently repeat the suggestions daily, but the main point is that you successfully deal with your problems, so even if your trance state is not as deep as you wish, this will not prevent you successfully using self suggestion.

Some people achieve their objectives without ever experiencing the trance state, so do not hold up your progress by waiting until you have achieved some preconceived idea of what the trance state should be. During each suggestion session make the following suggestions to yourself.

"I am going to deal conclusively with my problems once and for all."

"I will have the patience and the perseverance to keep on practising."

CHAPTER FIVE

ROUTINE OF SELF-SUGGESTION SESSION

In the preceding sections we have so far been concerned with certain instructions for relaxation routines and the suggestions given at the end of sections Three and Four.

Now you are ready for the next step. Having relaxed, lie down with your eyes closed and, under closed eyelids direct your eyes slightly upwards as though you were looking at a spot between your eyebrows. It may be found helpful to place a small object (a coin will do), in the centre of the forehead on which to concentrate. Whilst doing this the eyes must remain closed. Do not strain, but keep them directed in that position until it becomes an effort to do so. If you feel any strain or effort in maintaining this position of the eyes, just "let go" and rest. Don't do anything at all. Do not open your eyes. Don't bother to think about your eyes, they may move under your lids or they may not. If they want to move, let them. If they want to stay as they are, let them. Many people at this stage feel very detached. With continued practice, the feeling of detachment becomes deeper.

Do not let your mind begin analysing or reflecting on how you are progressing with your exercises while you are engaged in carrying them out.

Just launch yourself into the routine and submit or surrender yourself to the languid feeling which will result from carrying out the exercises.

You may begin to experience some degree of light trance at this stage, but the majority of people have to continue with further methods to heighten the state of suggestibility. Begin each session by relaxing and you will notice now, having carried out a daily practice session for a few weeks, you are able to achieve the relaxed state more rapidly. You will now be able to leave out the detailed attention to the arms, legs, etc.

As the next step in learning self suggestion and auto hypnosis the following method, is in my opinion a sound basic method to which you can add any variations you will later find helpful.

One, two, three, Method. This method can be used anywhere, any time. No preparation is required and there is no need to isolate oneself. On the lines described later in this section it may be practised in a restaurant, sitting in a bus, or during a few minutes at business. To describe this as a method seems over elaborate for once the ability "to sink into oneself" has been mastered, all that is necessary is the simple routine which follows. Take a few deep breaths, fix the eyes on some object such as an electric light switch or a door knob, and count "one, two, three" and at three let your eyes gently close. Continue counting softly to yourself up to "ten." When you get to "ten," direct your attention to your right thumb and mentally count again to ten, then transfer your attention to the first finger of your right hand and again count to "ten," then to the second finger and so with all the fingers on both hands. Count slowly and silently at a speed which does not leave time for other thoughts to break in whilst counting.

Take your time over the ritual of counting your fingers and when this is completed, direct your attention to your mouth and sense the feeling of your lips and tongue. It will help to locate this feeling if you slightly move your tongue. Following this direct your attention inwards as though to the spot between your eyes mentioned in the previous method.

Whilst you have been practising, subtle mental and physical changes will have been taking place quite automatically. If for example you were counting at the rate of one each second, by the time you had brought your awareness to the spot between your eyes, about two minutes would have passed since you began, and during that time with your eyes shut and your attention focused at a sensory level of awareness by the monotony of counting, a slow but subtle drift towards the trance state will have occurred.

Up till now you have had to isolate yourself to carry out your practice. Now you can take a big step forward by relaxing and administering suggestions to yourself wherever you may be.

In the previous exercises of relaxing your arms, legs, back, you have been practising differential relaxation, that is the relaxing of all muscles other than those actually necessary for the performance of any particular task. This ability is now applied to relaxing WHILST SEATED IN A CHAIR. The object of being able to carry out the General Relaxation exercise *whilst seated* is so that relaxation can be practised at any time without the necesity of lying down. Once general relaxation has been mastered whilst seated, it is possible to carry out self suggestion, on a train or bus, or wherever you may be, without anyone being aware of what you are doing.

If you intend carrying out self suggestion whilst seated, again go through the exercises of tensing the arms, tensing the legs and head lolling *whilst you are sitting*. Do this until you experience the same sensation of heaviness and relaxation which you have had whilst lying down.

This differential functioning can be performed, not only

by our muscles, but also by consciousness itself. A very good example is furnished by our hearing which is highly selective. It selects from the medley of sound in everyday life only those which, in some way, require our attention. Many noises, such as those of cars, clocks, voices, etc., are allowed to pass unnoticed without being brought to our conscious attention for the simple reason they are of no concern or interest to us.

After a few sessions the sensory appreciation of tension will be more clearly defined, and the ability to consciously "let go", physically and mentally, comes more under conscious control. Repeat each exercise until you are satisfied that you have made some progress, but do not expect anything dramatic or startling, just keep on producing the maximum feeling of detachment, ease and relaxation that you can. The effects of these exercises are cumulative and the degree of detachment which is attained is determined mainly by the regularity with which the exercises are carried out, and the absence of any *negative* self suggestion during or in between practice sessions.

At each session when you have carried out your relaxation routine let the suggestions with which this Section ends float through your mind. In relaxing you have been preparing your body and now with suggestions of this nature, you are mobilising inner resources which will aid you.

Profiting by Arjuna's experience, you can hasten your acquisition of the superior weapons (or techniques) which will enable you to conclusively deal with your problems by patiently plodding away on your daily suggestion sessions. You can get through from day to day with the weapons you have, but to win conclusively you may want superior weapons. These weapons (like Arjuna) you can acquire by asking for aid from the positive elements in your unconscious mind by suggestions of the following nature:

"One way or another I am going to get rid of my trouble/complaint/ailment" (mentioning whatever your objective may be).

"If it is necessary for me to gain further knowledge, I want my unconscious mind to work for me and help me to discover this knowledge."

"I am willing if necessary to change my methods . . . all I want to do is to solve my problem."

"With all my heart and soul I sincerely want to get rid of this problem once and for all and want all the help I can get."

Your work so far could be likened to preparing the ground and in the next Section we will begin to examine and choose the seeds (or suggestions) we wish to plant.

CHAPTER SIX

DEVISING THE RIGHT SUGGESTIONS

We will now consider how we can plan and devise more informed suggestions to pass on to the positive elements in our unconscious mind.

Most people beginning to learn self hypnosis are sure they know what suggestions they wish to make ... in most cases they are wrong. They know what they wish to achieve, but very few know the best suggestions to use to bring about what they desire. At the beginning of this Course I told the story of how Arjuna received unexpected help, and how by making suggestions similar to those I prescribed at the end of the last Session, unexpected aid will come from the unconscious mind. If we enlist its aid it will show us opportunities we have not previously seen; it will show us hidden obstacles and how they can be avoided; it will show us how to alter our attitude towards unalterable circumstances; it will quicken hope, free enthusiasms, and inspire us, but we must not, like Arjuna, let courage make us so cocksure that we think we can order the unconscious mind about. This cannot be done—but we can get its co-operation.

An excellent example of a good strategetical approach in using suggestion techniques was the case of a man who, although he never achieved any real depth of trance, cured himself of nervous tensions, fears, indifferent health, poor memory and gained promotion. He had been employed for many years as a clerk, though his knowledge and experience of the business fitted him for a far better position. Following the instructions in the Course he began by employing suggestions on the following lines—"I am going to use my abilities to the full, I am not going to be a slave to ill health, I am going to rid myself of whatever it is that holds me back. I am going to lose this nervousness. I want the courage to see if I am creating difficulties for myself. If I am I will find some way of dealing with them. I am going to get on at my work." He carried on with these suggestions for some days. Then one night he had a strange dream. He dreamed that one of the Directors of his business was coming towards him with a cheque in his hand, and he, the dreamer, turned and ran away from this Director, feeling very much afraid. Then he began to notice that at business he was very tense whenever this Director came into the office. He began to realise that unconsciously he was very much afraid of this Director and that this was the underlying reason for his mediocre performance at business. Unconsciously he was avoiding responsibility and promotion which would have brought him under this Director's immediate supervision. He continued with his suggestions and soon discovered that the Director's appearance was reminiscent of a school teacher who had bullied him unmercifully at school. Once the hidden cause of his tensions and fears came to consciousness he began to see the nature of the conflict and how he had previously been fighting to repress his fears and tensions. Once he saw the real underlying cause of his difficulties he carried on with self diagnostic suggestions, and day by day the energies which had been absorbed by the repressed fears were freed. He felt strangely relieved, and his suggestions "I know I can do a better job" had a ring of truth which would not have been the case had he begun with parrotlike suggestions of, "I have 100 per cent confidence." If he had used short sighted suggestion he would have repressed his fears and would have been fighting his unconscious mind instead of getting its co-operation. As will be seen in this example, the all important point is to gain the co-operation of the unconscious mind, by choosing the right suggestions and, if necessary, altering them.

Do not try to rush matters. If results are going to come quickly nothing will stop them, but to build up hopes of results immediately leaves one open to disappointment. The strategy I recommend is that the individual says to himself "I will do my best to keep up regular practice. If I can only improve one per cent a day I will not grumble, but I am going to get the co-operation of my unconscious mind as soon as I can. One thing is certain, I am going to deal with this (stating own problem). I am going to go on with it until I succeed and the job is finished." By adopting this attitude emotional ups and downs will be avoided, and in consequence, more rapid progress made.

Another important point in planning is to remember that we do not consciously invent or make up the suggestions. It is true we become aware of them in our conscious minds. But the desires for peace of mind, health and happiness all spring from the unconscious mind. They are the desires of the unconscious and if it is approached with sincerity and patience it will allow man to tap energies he never dreamed he possessed, carry out feats which seemed impossible and cure complaints which had been regarded as hopeless.

By becoming conscious of the contradictory impulses from within, and the influences from the outside world, and selecting and strengthening those which will enable us to achieve what we want the power to control ourselves is acquired. We are enabled to achieve these desired changes in ourselves because we can create, for a short time, the mental images and thoughts of the things we wish to achieve. In this way we can alter our lives by building new habits and attitudes, and thus re-direct the elemental energy of the instincts to the purposes of the will.

In life, until a man has achieved some knowledge of self, he stands at a crossroad. Ahead of him lie two divergent roads. One leads to all the things he fears and dreads, whilst the other is the road by which he can reach his ideals, his hopes and his higher aspirations. This is what Freud meant when he said that each man could reach heights he had never dreamt of, and could fall to depths he had never imagined. The framing of a man's suggestions are chosen from the things that he hopes, wishes and desires, and as soon as he begins consciously and consistently to practise self suggestions he begins to move positively and with certainty towards the things he most desires, and to leave his fears behind him.

Suggestions in the beginning can be of a very general nature. All that is necessary is that they are sincere, and the more simple and uncomplicated the better. A number of specimen suggestions are now given. They begin with suggestions which are designed to strengthen the resolution of the individual to continue the task he has begun in studying this Course, and to achieve his objectives.

"I will remember to carry out my exercises."

"I will make steady progress."

"I want to become more and more enthusiastic about altering my life."

"Every time I read or practise I will do my very best to make progress."

"I am willing to make whatever changes may be necessary in my life to attain what I desire."

"Each day I will work to be more self possessed and surer of myself."

"I want to get a bird's eye view of my life and see what is essential to my happiness and success."

"I will observe and be pleased with my successes, and I will learn from any setbacks."

"I will alter what is within my power to alter, and will change my attitude towards those things which I cannot change."

"My patience will increase every day, and things that used to disturb me will leave me unmoved."

"I shall not talk, think, or let my mind dwell on unpleasant, morbid subjects."

"I shall direct my thoughts towards pleasant things, and the sort of individual I should like to be."

"I shall be on my guard against what I know to be my weaknesses."

"I will see my past mistakes and try to avoid repeating them in the future."

"I will begin to see more clearly the obstacles which are preventing me from obtaining happiness, health and peace of mind, and how they may be overcome."

"If I suffer any disappointments or reverses this will not shake my faith in myself, or in the power of suggestion."

"I am going to be able to concentrate and to think more clearly."

"I am going to be able to remember things more easily. My memory will be more retentive."

"My self control and self possession and confidence is going to grow steadily."

"I am going to develop mental poise, and peace of mind."

"My ability to control my mental and emotional life is growing."

"I am going to enjoy better health and have more energy."

"Every day I will observe myself and every day I will try to learn something."

"I am going to be less tense and find it easier to relax."

"I am going to be more tolerant with other people, and try to understand their difficulties."

Take your own particular desires, disabilities or difficulties and express them in words. If, for example, you lack confidence say "I am going to get over these feelings. I am going to feel more confident every day. These suggestions will help to make me stronger and have more self control. I am not going to worry what other people think about me," and continue on these lines.

It will be noticed that many of the above suggestions refer to the future, such as: "I am going to feel more confident." This method of self suggestion employs the phenomena of post-hypnotic suggestion which, as readers who have witnessed a hypnotic demonstration, or who have read on the subject will know, is a form of delayed action suggestion. It operates by registering impressions directly on the subconscious mind, and they are carried out at a later date. The most common example of self administered post-hypnotic suggestion is when someone says to himself: "Tomorrow morning *I am going to wake up* at seven o'clock" If he does wake up at seven o'clock he has succeeded in giving himself a post-hypnotic suggestion. The ability to do this is an inherent faculty in everyone and it can be employed to alter one's future attitude, actions or thoughts and by this means many changes can be effected which cannot be effected by will power alone.

It cannot be over-emphasised that self suggestion and

self hypnotism are a means to an end, and the suggestions must be sound and reasonable and planned on a long-term policy if real lasting benefit is to follow. The majority of nervous breakdowns occur because people have success-fully suggested to themselves that they were capable of greater efforts than they were in reality able to carry out. They had used suggestion to stifle the warnings of their fatigue centres and drawn recklessly on their reserves of nervous energy until they collapsed. This is obviously not an intelligent use of self suggestion. It is necessary that the suggestions made to oneself should not make undue demands on one's body, but rather that they should aid the body through suggestions of sound sleep, alterations in diet, lowering of tensions, and intelligent direction of effort which will enable the body to work more efficiently.

The mistake of using the power of suggestion without carefully considering the nature of the suggestions made can be exemplified by the following story:—A hypnotist met a man who was very worried and asked why he looked so worried. The man replied: "I am very worried about my overdraft at the bank, it kept me awake last night and I can't bear the idea of spending any money." The hypno-tist said: "I'll soon fix that—sit down and relax." He then hypnotised the man and proceeded to give suggestions on the following lines: "You will forget all about your bank manager and all about your overdraft. When you wake up all your money troubles will have vanished. If you see anything in a shop which you want, you'll go right in and buy it." Everyone will see the fallacy of symptom removal in such a case, but it should be kept in mind that the same laws apply whether we are spending money or nervous energy for, in both cases, overdrafts cannot be indefinitely increased.

It was previously commented on that the things that we

wish to achieve are inherent strivings, or the expression of
the deepest aspirations of one's nature. The suggestions
prepared by one sincerely desiring to establish his life on
a sound basis, to help others, and to achieve peace of
mind, is almost identical with prayers which are also
addressed to the source of all life. This similarity is clearly
seen in one of the prayers of St. Francis of Assisi which
follows:

Lord make me an instrument of thy peace
Where there is hatred—let me sow love
Where there is doubt—let me sow faith
Where there is despair—let me sow hope
Where there is darkness—light
Where there is sadness—joy
O Divine Master grant that I do not so much seek
    to be consoled as to console—
    to be understood as to understand—
    to be loved as to love.
For it is in giving that we receive—
    in pardoning that we are pardoned—
    and in dying that we are born to everlasting
    life.

Self treatment suggestions aimed at achieving normal,
healthy functioning of the mind, body and emotions are
not alien demands imposed from outside. They are the
conscious expression of inherent desires from within. Unconscious activities superintend the electro-chemical
transformation of food and energy and the functions of
repairing and replacing broken or injured skin, bone and
tissue. In short, all the unconscious processes strive to
correct mal-functioning of all kinds, and to maintain or
regain health. This process can be assisted by conscious

suggestions. One of the most important factors in successful suggestions is the clear interpretation of these inherent strivings, the fusion of the conscious with the unconscious. This is the recognition of the healthy and constructive aims of the unconscious and their reinforcement by the conscious mind; this and the removal or circumvention of the resistances to this process are the main factors in successful suggestion. Self doubt, and forgetting to carry out regular suggestion sessions are the main obstacles.

In framing suggestions it is wisest, particularly in the initial stages, not to expect too much. Set a modest programme. If a difficulty has existed for some time, in all probability attempts to treat it will have already been made unsuccessfully. If this is so, the individual will, despite himself, have entertained negative suggestions. They can, however, be outweighed by regular positive suggestions. No one knows better than the individual himself his hopes and fears, the ways in which he desires to alter his life, and some of the circumstances which help and some of those which hinder him. Frame the suggestions of what you wish to accomplish. These desires should be expressed in clear, short, easily understood sentences.

Some of these suggestions will be of a personal nature, designed to fulfil your needs. They will probably deal with many aspects of your life such as diet, sleep, sex or personal habits, intimate associations with others, future plans and matters with which no one but you yourself are acquainted.

In the next Section we will deal with self observation which enables you to see and follow up the clues and guidance offered to you by your unconscious mind.

CHAPTER SEVEN

SELF OBSERVATION BETWEEN SUGGESTION SESSIONS

Self Observation means observing the way in which our suggestions have affected our behaviour. This self observation calls for frank self scrutiny, but is carried out solely for the purpose of discovering our mistakes so that we may avoid or overcome them.

Watch for the negative moods in yourself. When in these moods the most profitable observations can be made. For example, if a thought such as, "I am not making sufficient progress," occurs, do not repress it, do not conceal your doubts from yourself. Suggestion can rid you of them but you cannot put anything right until you know what it is that is wrong. Self honesty is necessary in observing oneself. It is no good attempting to concentrate on the bright side, and to pretend that the dark side does not exist. Repression is permissible as a temporary expedient and, in many cases, is a necessary measure to free our minds to carry on our everyday occupation, but, as a permanent policy it is disastrous for it succeeds only when our energy level is sufficiently high to inhibit or repress the unwanted thoughts, emotions and compulsions. Self observation or the observing of other people gives ample proof that until an individual has arrived at a certain stage in development, self control is lessened through shocks, fatigue and illness. Courage, endurance and will power are needed to repress difficulties, doubts and fears, but courage of a different order is required to be frank with ourselves, and to admit our limitations. It might appear that to admit one's limitations, doubts and fears, would cause one to lose ground, but in actual fact through frank admission of our limitations comes strength of a new order. We no longer make impossible demands upon ourselves. We can afford to take reverses. It is no longer a question to "do or die." A negative mood, a shock or some reverse is an episode and not a major defeat once one acquires this wider and more flexible strategy. When we gain a more realistic appraisal of our strengths and weaknesses, we can extend a new tolerance to ourselves and to others (for we cannot be kind to others until we can be kind to ourselves). With this alteration in our attitude we can view our shortcomings, with tolerance, for criticism must be kind to be constructive.

In observing oneself whilst carrying on the day's work note the incidents which affect you adversely, whether they be people, your own thoughts, actions, foods, incidents or any other circumstances. A sound method, is to write down the next two incidents which annoy or irritate you, the next two which make you sad, the next two which create tension, the next two which make you feel pleased with yourself. If something causes you to be tense, afraid, annoyed, pleased, reflect and ask yourself questions about this reaction. "Why did I feel like that?" "At whom, or at what, was the feeling directed?" "What caused the emotion or physical disturbance?" These reactions reveal the hidden character structure which can only be learned by these devious approaches. Self observation is strictly practical work which can be aided by asking oneself questions such as: "What is the biggest mistake I have made today?" "What have I learned today?" etc.

In watching for results from the suggestions you have given yourself, it is important to remember that there is frequently a time lag between suggestions being given and their fulfilment. Sometimes it is necessary to continue suggestions for some time before their effects are noticed, for frequently inner resistances have to be overcome. If it were not for this fact all suggestions, both good and bad, would become immediately effective.

Be on your guard for a short time after having successfully achieved a change in habit. In an unguarded moment, before the new habit has become firmly established, it is easy to slide back. Carry on with your suggestions for a few days in order to consolidate the position. For example, if someone, through suggestion, had given up smoking, it would be wise for a few days to continue to suggest: "I have given up smoking and *will not* smoke again. I will *not be* caught off my guard when someone offers me a cigarette. I *will not* be talked into smoking," etc.

The purpose of observing oneself is to note the changes which you have effected in yourself as a result of your self suggestions. Note the improvements and benefits you have achieved, as these evidences of successful self suggestion make further advances easier and also consolidate the improvements made and bed them down into permanent habits. Where your self suggestions have not met with the success you anticipated, do not let this discourage you. The technique of suggestion is something to be learned, and is one in which the beginner, as in any other subject will have failures. Where there are failures, change the type of suggestion, approach your objective from another angle.

The intelligent application of Self Suggestion calls for careful thought and constant revision of suggestions. It is a means to an end. You are the only one who knows the particular difficulties and problems with which you are faced, the disabilities, habits and attitudes of which you wish to rid yourself, and the life you desire to live in the future. To attain these ends it may be necessary for you to frequently reshape your suggestions guided by what is learned during self observation.

As a result of self observation some people find that they have not the time to carry out exercises. Others find that they forget to carry them out. If these obstacles arise— then some action should be taken. It is only by facing facts that we can alter ourselves. It must not be forgotten that the majority of resolutions that people make are forgotten, for the line of least resistance is to do today what we did yesterday, and most likely we will do the same tomorrow. Habits are strong, and some persistence in effort is necessary if we are to effect changes in ourselves. If you should suddenly realise that you have forgotten to carry out an exercise or something you had planned, close your eyes and mentally repeat, very rapidly, to yourself: "I will not forget . . . I will not forget . . . I will not forget." Spend a minute or two doing this. It is also a very sound idea to fall back on mechanical reminders, such as carrying round written instructions to oneself, or to carry out waking suggestions at certain times,—before every meal, when you get up, before going to sleep, every time the sun goes down, or, if you are indoors, when the lights are switched on. Two minutes waking suggestion three or four times a day will effect a great deal of influence on one's life if one is sincere in desiring what one asks for. Obviously suggestions would, in cases of forgetfulness, be directed towards curing this shortcoming which could, if allowed to go unchecked, bring your efforts to effect alterations in yourself through this course to a standstill. In cases such as this, suggestions would be on the following lines: "I am not going to forget," "I will remember more easily in future." "From now on I shall do my practice more regularly."

If your self suggestion has for a while been progressing well and you seem to come to a standstill, or to have set-backs, there will be reasons for this. Try to find them out. It may be caused by a chill, a slight indisposition, the result of unusual physical or mental efforts, a disruption of one's affairs, or some temporary disturbances. These changes may produce temporary setbacks, and should be taken into account. Planned suggestions directed specific-ally towards them can do much to ameliorate or offset these disturbances. Sometimes people encounter setbacks because they attempt to progress too rapidly, and if the individual tries to force himself, or to progress too rapidly, unconscious resistances may come into operation. The changes which are being produced by suggestion are a natural process, and the time taken to effect them varies according to the difficulties, inner resistances, strength of existing habits and particular circumstances in the life of each individual. The golden rule in suggestion technique is NO FORCING. Gentle persistence is the keynote.

If something disturbs or upsets you during the day, having taken what practical action you can to deal with the incident, its possible consequences, and to prevent its repetition, put the matter from your mind, for suggestions dealing with the matter can be framed later when you are replanning your suggestions. To banish difficulties from one's mind consciously is not necessarily a harmful repres-sion, for, in other words, there are "permissible repres-sions."

Whatever progress you make with trance induction, at every opportunity use waking suggestions, as the object of the self suggestion techniques is not to conduct one's life by carrying out a series of post hypnotic suggestions, but by the integration of the unconscious activities with the conscious, intellectual activities.

Remarkable though the powers of Self Suggestion and Self Hypnotism may be, they are powerless to alter many conditions of life. They cannot bring back our youth, or those we have lost, nor can they make good irreparable physical damage, but through these powers of self suggestion we can rise above the inevitable changes that are caused by the passing of time BY ALTERING OUR ATTITUDE TOWARDS THOSE CIRCUMSTANCES WHICH WE ARE POWERLESS TO CHANGE.

We have so far dealt with a method of relaxation and the first steps in self suggestion. These two techniques are combined in the self suggestion session which you are now carrying out. Later we will be dealing with more advanced methods of trance induction, but first we must give some attention to the way in which we register suggestions in the unconscious mind.

CHAPTER EIGHT

REGISTERING SUGGESTIONS IN THE UNCONSCIOUS MIND

There are certain basic desires in everyone which strive for self expression. If they remain unexpressed the individual becomes frustrated, for his life force is strangled back. It is here suggested that these desires, whether they be a desire for better health, more confidence, more friends, success in some undertaking, or the ability to help others, should be expressed and made articulate in the form of suggestions. Throughout the ages people have striven in various ways to express their inner needs. They have wished, hoped, prayed and used self suggestion, and the more simply and sincerely they have been able to do so, the more successfully have their wishes come to fruition.

Registering suggestions in the unconscious mind actually requires very little effort . . . if the preparatory work on relaxation has been done and what you are going to suggest has been previously decided.

Having isolated yourself from the outside world and directed the attention inwards, allow yourself to mentally drift away from the world of sight and sound into an inner world. In a dreamy, detached fashion carry out the trance induction routine of counting, and noting the heaviness of the body and other sensations of detachment. This should go on automatically. There is a complete submission to the sensation of drifting and to effortlessly repeating silently to oneself, "I am sinking down . . . further . . . further" (or whatever formula you are using). Surrender to this experience. Reason is stilled and becomes a silent spectator to this feeling and experience of floating detachment.

Gradually this sensation of sinking will come to a point where it seems to stop and one remains stationary . . . poised as it were, vaguely aware, but with nothing happening. This is just as it should be . . . the will, present but not being exercised. Rather like a shepherd, who, effortlessly resting on the hillside, sees all the movements of his flock and his awareness is in the role of a passive witness. This is approaching the borderland separating the conscious from the unconscious mind, to go beyond this point, means that control would be lost. This is the point when suggestions will be registered in the unconscious mind. This is achieved by letting your suggestions float through your mind.

Exercises in the Course to create this state can be likened to the tilling of the ground . . . and the act of registering self suggestions, to the planting of seeds. If the ground has been well tilled, i.e. if the relaxation exercises have been carried out, and the formulation or reflection on suggestions also carried out, the registering of the desired instructions upon the unconscious mind will not be difficult. It is essential that no effort is exerted when making self suggestions. If the judgment begins analysing what is occurring, the process of registering ideas in the unconscious mind is immediately brought to a standstill. It is as though, after planting seeds the gardener were to dig up the tiny, fragile seedlings to see how they are growing. The result would probably be to destroy the plants before they had time to establish themselves. It is the absence of any intellectual interference, which enables suggestions to take root in the unconscious mind. The success of suggestion is dependent on by-passing the conscious mind and registering the desired impression directly on the unconscious mind.

If we are sufficiently absorbed in anything we forget everything else and become completely immersed in it. No effort is necessary to give attention to an interesting book, a TV or radio programme. It holds our whole attention.

Many people feel that they cannot give the same sustained attention to carrying out exercises on relaxation, trance induction and self suggestions as they would to an interesting book or film. Concentration is largely a matter of interest, but what would the man who feels he cannot concentrate reply if he were asked: "ARE YOU INTERESTED IN FEELING PHYSICALLY AND MENTALLY FIT? ARE YOU INTERESTED IN LEAVING ALL YOUR TROUBLES AND DIFFICULTIES BEHIND YOU?" Not only will he be interested, but as soon as he can see a practical way of achieving fitness and freedom from worry, he will do all he can to attain them.

Waking suggestions are carried out by repetition and can be made to oneself at any time. It does not matter where you are, standing, walking, or sitting once the technique is grasped it is no longer necessary to isolate oneself. In the beginning it is necessary to have the most favourable conditions, but later all this is unnecessary. Many people who have mastered self suggestion never go into a trance to register suggestions in their minds. All they do is close their eyes and register the desired suggestion. It would have value if the reader pauses at the end of this paragraph and says to himself (and means it) " I *am* going to learn how to get more control over my mind ... I *am* going to do this."

It is a good practice to carry out waking suggestions

regularly by setting a fixed time for making them to one-self. For example, every lunch time set aside a few minutes. Similarly use as a cue, or reminder, some happening such as when the electric light goes on, or when you glance at your watch, and at each of these times give yourself a few waking suggestions. All that is necessary is to close your eyes and count three and impress the suggestion on your mind, open your eyes and carry on with whatever you were doing. The more often you do this the more effectively your suggestions will be registered.

Some people repeat waking suggestions to themselves over and over again as they lie in bed before going to sleep. One method of self suggestion is to write down suggestions on a piece of paper, and last thing at night read it ten times, then place the paper under the pillow and sleep on it. Or another to write out suggestions for the day, and carry them around in one's pocket. It is a good idea to write out the week's suggestions in one's diary. It is also a useful device to write out suggestions in the form of a letter and post it to oneself and when receiving it to read and re-read several times.

Implanting suggestions in the mind is like planting seeds in a garden. Just as it is necessary to keep a garden clear of weeds, it is in a similar fashion necessary to keep the mind clear of negative thoughts.

Do not always repress doubts, try to trace what has caused them, to see if they arise from some matter which requires your attention.

Before turning to the next section, let us pause to review the method employed in this course. It is not advocated that you should relax and repeat the same suggestions every day. Once the method is grasped you will find it becomes interwoven into all your thinking, wishing, and planning. This does not mean you will be day-dreaming or suggesting to yourself all day, but it does mean a new kind of informed awareness in thinking about yourself, your plans and in observing yourself and other people, and instead of chance or negative reactions, you will find you have positive reactions which are the result of your following a programme.

The programme is as follows:

PLANNING
SUGGESTIBLE STATE (creation of)
REGISTERING SUGGESTIONS IN UNCONSCIOUS MIND
SELF OBSERVATION
REPLANNING SUGGESTIONS

Some of these different phases though described separately, are performed simultaneously. They are not as easy to separate in practice, as they are in theory, for example the deepening of the trance state, and the self administration of suggestions are sometimes carried out at the same time, also Self Observation and the Replanning of Suggestions will often be more or less part of the same act.

The system of self suggestion is a programme, in which positive thoughts are guided and monitored towards making definite changes in one's life, instead of drifting or letting chance or the past determine what happens. The whole cycle is ceaselessly repeated ... Planning, Suggestion Sessions, Self Observation, Amending of, or adding to Suggestions.

CHAPTER NINE

THE SELF HYPNOTIC TRANCE

The creation of the self hypnotic state has been a practice since the earliest times. In most esoteric writings the importance of self induced trances has been stressed as a method of curing ills and gaining knowledge.

Much of the work in Yoga is concerned in ultimately being able to enter a self induced trance. This is preceded by purification of the body, inside and out, by maintaining physical postures (asanas), by breathing exercises (pranayama) and by mental concentration. In the Bhagavad Gita, Chapter 5, verses 27 and 28 is the following instruction:

"Shutting out all external objects, fixing the vision between the eyebrows, making even, the inward and outward breaths, moving between the nostrils, the sage who has controlled the senses, the mind and understanding. . . ."

Trance states are self induced by many people all over the world. Some believe that they are making contact with Gods, or with their ancestors' spirits, or that it is a form of magic. In the West self hypnosis is being increasingly regarded in a much more factual way, namely as a method of contacting the unconscious mind.

Although the basic principles underlying the techniques of self hypnotism and successful trance induction are the same in any part of the world, local conditions are not and these make a great deal of difference to trance induction. The mental state is dependent on the chemistry of

the body. Too much oxygen makes us lose control of ourselves and with too little we become insensible. Altitude
is also a real factor. In Johannesburg, at 6,000 feet above
sea level, motor cars from lower altitudes need a car-
burettor adjustment. When we find the gross mechanism
of a car can be affected by the altitude it is not surprising
that the chemistry of the body and the mental operations
can also be affected. Mountains and deserts are traditional
places of retreat for meditational purposes. From my
experience the greater the altitude the easier the trance
induction and this I believe is something quite apart from
the amount of oxygen in the air. Some people enter a
trance more easily when they have less than average oxygen in their bloodstream, and others succeed more easily
when they have more than the average amount of oxygen.
This is a matter which the reader must find out for himself. Before practice sessions I would recommend trying
very shallow breathing for a minute before carrying out
practice in your relaxation or trance induction. Then at
another time try deep breathing. In subsequent sessions
use deep breathing or shallow breathing, whichever suits
you best.

The variations between individuals and their own local
conditions make it impossible to lay down any hard and
fast instructions to suit everyone.

There are many states of consciousness, but the average
individual has probably not considered such a matter. It is
not as though man is either awake or asleep, or that he is
either conscious or unconscious. There is no such simple
division. There are many intermediate states and, in fact,
when we are asleep we are not really unconscious. For
example, if someone were to break a window in a room in
which the reader was sleeping he would wake up with a
start, and in his sleep he would have heard the tinkle of

the broken glass...and yet he was asleep when the window was broken. Actually he was not completely unconscious. A part of the mind remains on duty as a sentinel even when we are asleep. If there is anything unusual, a sound, or a smell of burning, the sentinel will wake us. There are a number of these different trance states which can be cultivated. In some the will is in abeyance but can be brought into operation to register the suggestions we wish in the unconscious mind. These states are difficult to describe, but if the reader will carry out the instructions and will co-operate by experimenting to find the best methods, he will soon discover that in this way he can gain a vastly increased control over himself.

There are various methods of increasing suggestibility and of hypnotising oneself. The most commonly used method is the Fixed Gaze, of which there are a number of variations, some of which are described in the following section.

It is advisable when beginning to put into operation the methods which follow, not to hold up progress by comparing the feelings you will experience with preconceived ideas about "going off." If a bowl of jelly is shaken at intervals while it is setting, and at each shaking the comment is made: "It doesn't look as if it was going to set," under these circumstances the jelly is very unlikely to ever set. Similarly with suggestion—if whilst carrying out exercises you are also mentally making a running commentary, progress is likely to be delayed.

The state of suggestibility differs with different people. Do not set the condition that you must go into a trance at once. There's only one way to judge the results of suggestion and that is by results. There is an Eastern proverb: "Drop by drop the pitcher is filled" No suggestions, or prayers or good efforts are ever lost. Although you may not see dramatic results from your suggestion sessions immediately even if you create only the lightest of trances or were only relaxing and using autosuggestion some of your suggestions will register in your unconscious mind where they will become an accumulating force.

It is sound strategy to say to yourself: "I am in no hurry about this. I am not going to prejudice the whole undertaking by setting a date when I should go into a trance, or when I should achieve what I want." You are an individual and every individual is different. You may achieve what you want easily and rapidly or you may have a difficulty of long standing which may take some time to deal with. Do not set any time limit. Simply devote what time you can to practice, even if it is only a few minutes a day, and steadily go ahead on the lines suggested.

In many cases people write and tell me that they have achieved what they want without any appreciable depth of trance. They merely followed the instructions, making self suggestions on the lines advocated in the Course during relaxation sessions.

Once you have acquired the art of putting suggestion into the unconscious mind it is, in fact, not necessary to lie down and go through the relaxation routine before making suggestions to yourself. Successful self suggestion can be carried out while walking, standing, in a car or bus or wherever you may be. When you have mastered the art of self suggestion you can give your unconscious mind a directive, or order without going into a trance, simply by closing your eyes for a few moments and mentally speaking to yourself. When you come to carry out the Trance Induction methods choose one which appeals to you and begin to experiment with it. Then try others if you wish. The methods may be tried in any order. If the first one suits you there is no need to try any of the others.

I recommend the reader to experiment—to make altera
tions and create the best possible conditions for himself
according to his personal idiosyncrasies, the time he has
available and his environmental circumstances.

Before beginning your suggestion sessions make
arrangements for your comfort as already described. Pay
particular attention to the temperature of the room and
see that you will not be cold and there are no draughts . . .
later on these precautions are unnecessary. Before you
actually begin start off with waking suggestions. Say to
yourself, either aloud or mentally, "I am going to begin
hypnotising myself." The reason for using the word
"begin" is because you may not succeed at once and you
are guarding yourself against disappointment by avoiding
making an issue of success in a single session. If for any
reason you do not wish to hypnotise yourself but wish to
master the art of successful self suggestion say "I am going
to increase my suggestibility to the utmost without letting
myself go into a trance."

These preliminary waking suggestions should be direc-
tives for pre-determining your attitude during the suggestion session. The waking suggestions you should give
should be instructions suited to the circumstances and
practical arrangements for your session. For example "I
am going to spend X minutes and will let myself drift off
as far as possible . . . I will not criticise my efforts. If there
are any interruptions, telephone calls, if someone knocks
on the door or calls me, I will immediately rouse myself
and will become fully alert."

In the next section various methods of trance induction
are described.

CHAPTER TEN

INDUCING THE SELF HYPNOTIC TRANCE

This is a method of inducing self-hypnosis by fixing the gaze on some object, a door knob or a light switch, a candle or lamp. If using electric light the possibility of damage to the eyes should be avoided by using a low-wattage bulb, or shading the light. The procedure to be followed is to sit some six to ten feet from the object, candle or light and to relax physically—on the lines of the relaxation previously given—and direct one's gaze upon the object or light. Gaze steadily at the spot—let the image of what you are looking at register on your mind, and continue to look at it steadily. Disregard all ideas and sensations which may present themselves, such as noises, awareness of your own breathing, etc. You will become aware that your body is becoming heavier, and that you are becoming drowsier, and that your eyes will feel as though they are going to close. When it becomes too much of an effort to keep them open, let them close. If your mind remains alert and is analysing your progress, it will automatically bring the process of "letting go" to a stop. You must clear your mind—and keep it clear. Whatever noises occur do your best to disregard them—thoughts may drift into your mind, but gently push them out, and continue to let yourself rest and to become drowsier.

If the reader can obtain a crystal ball, set it on a stand, or hold it in the hands and regard it steadily with half-closed eyes. Similar results can be obtained by using a plain glass filled with water, or with a mirror. The same principles apply in each case. The lack of any specific point in distance on which to fix the eyes causes a slight disorientation, first of eye focus, and then of consciousness. This disorientation or detachment increases with suggestion. In the case of a crystal the "depth of focus" will be the diameter of the crystal, as is also the case with a tumbler of water or, in the case of a mirror, the thickness of the glass. This can be seen if a mirror is closely examined. The mirror is silvered on the back of the glass. Thus, whilst gazing at the mirror, particularly if this is done from the angle of approximately 45 degrees, it will be found that the eyes are sometimes fixed on the surface of the mirror, that is, the front surface of the glass, or sometimes on the silver surface, which is the back of the glass, or sometimes wandering midway between these two planes. The effect produced by this method can produce a number of different reactions. Some people experience drowsiness, some may go off into a trance.

For this method, obtain a mirror and in the centre paste a small piece of white paper, about the size of a pea. If a hand mirror is being used, lay it flat on the table so that you can look into it easily, and without strain. If the mirror of a dressing table is being used, seat yourself comfortably and look steadily at the spot you have pasted on it. Push all other thoughts out of your mind, and remain gazing intently at the spot. Do not let your attention wander. The distance of the spot from your eyes should be one that is comfortable and causes no strain. It is better if the head and body lean forward slightly, so that the eyes have to look upwards a little. Soon your eyes will blink or grow heavy. If they remain fixedly open they will begin to smart and burn, and your vision will become blurred. Just continue gazing at the focal point and soon a strong desire to close your eyes will be felt. Do nothing—*don't think or try to analyse what is happening.* The point is reached when your eyes will close of their own accord—when this happens, let them remain closed and rest, and drowsiness will get deeper and deeper. Let it increase to the utmost point which is consistent with the retention of sufficient control to rouse yourself if you wish to break the trance. Having arrived at this state, continue to rest.

Another method is to lie down relaxed, having previously arranged for some small object such as a bright bead, a key or a button, to be suspended about a foot from one's face. This can be arranged by tying a piece of string or thread across the room from a window-catch to a picture-rail directly over where you are lying or sitting. A further string or thread should then be attached to hang vertically. At the end of this string suspend the small object, which should be in front of, or slightly above, your eye-level so that the eyes look upwards and converge slightly.

Regard the object steadily until the induced heaviness and drowsiness causes the eyes to close, then continue to let yourself become drowsier.

There are many other ways of employing this method of gaze fixation for trance induction. Almost any object will serve the purpose of acting as a fixed point on which you can focus both your eyes and your attention.

There are various mechanical aids to learning self hypnosis, amongst which the fixed gaze contrivances such as revolving disks, lights, etc. can be helpful in the early stages of trance induction. The visual aids have the limitation of becoming inoperative after the eyes are closed, and it is here that the auditory aids such as listening to a metronome, or a clock ticking have the advantage by maintaining a link with the student through his sense of hearing.

Undoubtedly the most helpful aid is a recorded hypnotic induction in which the student is conditioned and guided by the hypnotist through the lighter trance states into a deeper trance. As the student can listen to the recording whenever and as often as he wishes the hypnotic conditioning is under his own control. A recorded course by the author is available which contains a hypnotic induction and post hypnotic suggestions that the student will subsequently be able to induce the trance state in himself without the aid of the recording. Further details about these recordings and where they are available may be obtained by writing to the author.

From my own experience the best and most convenient way of entering the trance state is an extension of the method described as the One, Two, Three Method described in Chapter Five. This can be carried out lying down or seated in a chair.

It will be found that if the previous instructions have been carried out by mentally counting One, Two, Three, the reflex will have been built where the eyes gently close by themselves at the count of Three, then with the eyes closed continue four, five, six, seven, eight, nine, ten. Whilst counting a drift will have occurred towards the trance state. This can be deepened by one of the following disorientation exercises.

When you have arrived at "ten" whilst resting, and your eyes close, direct your attention to the top right hand corner of the ceiling behind you. Pause for a few seconds, then direct your attention to the right hand corner of the room in front of you, to the front left hand corner, then behind left hand corner and back to the starting point. As we are positioned in space and time through our senses when we close our eyes and begin these disorientation exercises our mental appreciation begins to drift towards a trance or sleep state, and in this trance state you can make suggestions to yourself.

If the reader has attained only a light trance up to now, do not let him draw any negative conclusions about the ultimate outcome of his exercises. It cannot be repeated too often that suggestions can be effectively registered even in a very light trance.

The reader can now begin repeating suggestions to aid him in "letting go." Let him phrase general suggestions of ease—of being comfortable—of relaxing—of sinking down—of getting drowsier and drowsier—sleepier and sleepier, etc.

Another simple but effective method is to sit, or lie down and, when generally relaxed, begin slowly to count mentally to yourself. At the word "One" gently allow the eyes to close. At "Two" lazily open them. At "Three" close, and on "Four" open again. Continue counting and allowing the eyes to gently close on the odd numbers and opening them on the even numbers. When opening and closing the eyes do not do so jerkily but softly, letting them close, as it were, by themselves, and opening them smoothly and lazily. Before starting this method of induction, make the suggestion to yourself that your eyes are going to get heavier and heavier as you proceed, and before you have been counting very long they will be so heavy that it will be too much of an effort to open them. Continue counting until this occurs, and continue with suggestions as described in previous method.

CHAPTER ELEVEN

TRANCE INDUCTION (Continued)

Feed Back Method

This method is based on the fact that we ourselves are the best judge of the phrases or words which describe our inner sensations.

To operate this method, either write down or remember the phrases or words, which were helpful in carrying out exercises. The phrases which seemed to "ring a bell." Maybe "Feel heavier ... warmer ... my breathing is getting deeper". . . and so on. This method, when relaxed is to re-present to yourself as mental suggestions the feelings and sensations of relaxation and drowsiness which you have previously experienced. Frame these suggestions in such a manner as to intensify the effects; for example: "I am feeling heavier and heavier ... I am feeling warmer ... breathing getting deeper, the deeper my breathing and the heavier I feel the drowsier I am becoming." To operate, seat yourself or lie down as previously described, and make the suggestions to yourself. When making the suggestions to yourself it is not necessary to speak them aloud; to repeat them mentally is sufficient. As this detachment grows, the reader will be growing nearer and nearer to the position where he is playing the dual role of hypnotist and subject.

Reading Method

This is a simple method of flooding the mind with one idea to the exclusion of everything else. It consists of writing down some descriptions of relaxation based on how you felt during your previous inductions. Choose all sensations and feelings which are conducive to furthering complete relaxation. As a suggested beginning, something on these lines might be employed: "I am sitting comfortably and am feeling at ease. I am resting and feeling very drowsy—If I go on reading this I shall get drowsier—My arms feel heavy and my body feels heavier—I am reading more slowly—My eyelids are getting heavier—I find it an effort to read. My eyes are getting heavier and I am beginning to feel sleepy—I am feeling very comfortable—My body is relaxed—My arms are relaxed—My legs feel heavy—My feet and legs feel relaxed, and heavy. All the while I am becoming more comfortable—and more deeply relaxed—I just want to rest—-My eyes are getting heavier —So very heavy that I am closing them gradually. I want them to close—I just want to rest."

When you are going to employ this method for induction see that it is written clearly, or typed so that it can be read easily and without effort. Seat yourself comfortably, preferably with a low light, and read it slowly. Read slowly as you become affected by the suggestions. When your eyes want to close, let them, and allow yourself to rest for a few seconds—continue to make mental suggestions of detachment and then register your current suggestions.

Saturation of the Attention Method

This method consists of completely saturating the mind with one idea. To make the procedure clear, it has already been explained that there are a number of different elements present in any state of mind, or that consciousness is an aggregate of many elements. This method consists of a number of separate processes which are practised, one by one, beforehand. The induction then becomes a matter of performing all the separate processes simultaneously. If this is successfully carried out, the utmost state of detachment consistent with retention of volition is achieved.

To operate this method, take the idea of drowsiness as the one with which we wish to flood the mind. Drowsiness is chosen because it closely resembles the detached state of mind which the reader wishes to produce in himself.

The first process is the physical disposition of the body, as already dealt with in the first exercises on General Relaxation. The second process is to call to mind the general effects of drowsiness on the emotional state, its pleasantness, disinclination to make effort, its detachment, etc., which will already have been experienced in previous exercises. For the third process, visualise in the mind's eye the word DROWSINESS, as if it were printed in block letters on a piece of card, or, alternatively, if when experimenting you find it more efficacious, in your mind's eye picture yourself sitting comfortably nearly asleep. For the fourth process practise saying the word DROWSINESS OR DROWSY softly to yourself. In doing this feel the movements of the lips and tongue as you say it. Say it softly, slowly, lazily; say the words slowly. Mumble it if you wish. For the fifth process, bring the sense of hearing consciously into play. Listen to yourself saying the word "Drowsy" or "Drowsiness," listen closely to each syllable.

The next step is to see that the word "Drowsiness" is spoken as the act of breathing out is being made. See that the breathing out of the word becomes a sleepy sigh. These processes must, as far as possible, be practised separately until they can be performed without effort or thought.

Preliminary practice will be necessary to produce and marshal all these separate reflexes so that they may be smoothly co-ordinated, without any reference to, or supervision from, the conscious mind. We cannot expect to get any trance conditions until the conscious mind is perfectly free from these supervisory tasks. Attempts to induce auto-hypnosis will fail until the conscious mind is free from the task of arranging these psycho-physical conditions, for the simple reason that it is an impossibility to keep the mind a blank and think of something at the same time.

When the reflexes have become automatic, the conscious mind then becomes a passive spectator of what is happening. This is the detachment that is felt and experienced when auto-hypnosis is about to be induced.

When carrying out this induction, sit or lie down, and relax, then begin gently and quietly saying the word Drowsy or Drowsiness ... Feel the physical movements you are making with your tongue, lips, and those caused by your breathing ... Hear yourself saying the words softly ... In the mind's eye call up the picture you have chosen which is most strongly associated with drowsiness, i.e. the word printed on a card, or whatever mental picture you wish ... Physically feel all the sensations of the suggested idea.

Continue this process, but each time the word is uttered, speak it more slowly, say it more softly, and let the intervals between saying it get longer and longer. It is, of course, not necessary to say it with every outgoing breath. If this process of co-ordination is carried out, without any distractions, the whole mind, body and feelings will be subject to this one compulsive influence.

If the reader has conscientiously carried out the previous exercises he will have induced some degree of detachment, or trance condition. Even if only a light trance has been attained. give yourself suggestions that subsequent exercises will be successfully carried out, and the trance will become deeper.

Proceed without undue effort or haste. If results are slow in coming, face the fact. Follow the instructions carefully and conscientiously. Your progress may be rapid, or it may be slow. If the latter is the case, do not in any way be disturbed. If the exercises previously given are approached with the right attitude of mind, and are carefully carried out, it will not be long before sufficient detachment is achieved to successfully employ suggestion. By applying the re-presentation methods already described, a light trance can be steadily deepened.

Each of the methods described has terminated with the instruction to continue to become drowsier, or to rest. The depth of auto-hypnotic trance which is of the greatest value is that in which there is the maximum degree of detachment consistent, with retention of volition and "self control." It is a state in which the will is voluntarily suspended but sufficient volition is retained to terminate the trance if desired.

CHAPTER TWELVE

TRANCE DEEPENING

It is not at all necessary for the average reader wishing to cure some ailment, or to alter some condition or habit in his life, to master the trance deepening methods described in this section. I would emphasise that beneficial results are dependent on regular suggestions sessions, and frequent and realistic revisions of the suggestions. The methods in this section are primarily for students of psychological techniques, research, E.S.P. or meditational techniques, but many readers may wish to experiment with them.

The main causes which prevent trance induction, or the deepening of trances are:—trying too hard and being over anxious, employing induction methods which are not suitable to you, because your unconscious mind does not approve of the suggestions you wish to make, because unthinkingly you may have been making negative suggestions about your progress, or some form of unconscious resistance. The majority of these resistances can be overcome by following the advice given in this Course. In it, there is a great deal of information and instruction, but some readers may have to experiment with the various methods of trance induction described, perhaps making some alterations or modifications, or combining some of the different methods to find one which is suited to their individual circumstances and requirements.

When you experience only a slight feeling of detachment during practice, that is the time to make suggestions to yourself: your trance, however slight, will become deeper by using it, that is by repeating it and using positive suggestions. Do not say to yourself "This is not what I expected. This is not deep enough, I want a deep trance." Do not make it a condition that you must go into a deep trance before you begin suggestions. Remember that in any case the trance itself is only a means to an end, also remember that the majority of cures achieved by hypnotism are effected in medium and light trances. If you make it a definite condition that you must go into a deep trance it means you are, in effect, hypnotising yourself with the idea "I cannot get benefit until I go into a deep trance." This is untrue and there is no point in misleading yourself. The correct suggestion should be "Whether the trance I achieve is light, medium or deep I am going to get rid of (mention your difficulty) as soon as I possibly can." Do not lay down conditions. One of the main reasons for the resistance of the unconscious mind to trance induction is because the individual tries to force his unconscious mind. The way to deepen trances and one of the ways in which unconscious resistances are overcome is to make the right suggestions with gentle persistence . . . do this, and the trance will become deeper by itself. If you try to force matters you will arrive at a deadlock.

A very light trance can be created by simply closing the eyes and mentally counting up to ten. Given the right conditions this trance will become progressively deeper, but, if immediately after the "ten" the individual says to himself "I am not in a trance. I am wide awake, he automatically brushes aside what would have developed into a trance. If instead of making the above mental comment to himself he had mentally noted a heaviness in his arms or legs (refer to the relaxation exercises given earlier) and had mentally said "I believe my arms are getting heavier and my breathing seems a little deeper," and if he had continued in this strain, the light trance would have become progressively deeper.

I met a man in India who performed some very impressive feats and I commented on the ease and speed, with which he induced a trance in himself. I was surprised by his telling me, that it was seven years from the time he first tried to induce a trance, before he succeeded. The reason for his taking this long time was because at his first attempts he had an expectation of being able to create a trance in a few sessions. When he failed to induce a trance fairly quickly, he was disappointed and lost heart and gave up his attempts for the time being. For some years he tried at intervals without success to induce a trance until he realised that his failure was because he had unthinkingly been making negative suggestions to himself and he had not been systematically practising but had simply been carrying out desultory experiments when he felt like it. Once he began to practise regularly, he soon succeeded.

Sometimes, as in the case of the man just mentioned, a student may come to a standstill and not know why. It may be that he has encountered some form of unconscious resistance or for some other reasons.

It is not possible, in a general course of this nature, to give precise instructions in every case, but if he is not making the progress his efforts merit and cares to write, giving brief details to me c/o The Publishers. I will be pleased to advise the best steps to take to overcome his difficulty.

With the majority of people deepening trance is a gradual process, but with patience and perseverance most resistances gradually resolve themselves. One cause of resistance to trance induction is that the unconscious mind takes exception to the nature of the suggestions made by the conscious mind. Often by altering the suggestions this unconscious resistance is overcome. For example, suppose a man is behind with his work and is overworking, if he begins to make suggestions to overcome feelings of fatigue and he is already drawing too deeply on his reserves of energy, his unconscious mind will veto his suggestions and he will have an unconscious resistance to trance and hypnotic suggestion. If this applies to any reader he will find the solution by re-reading the recommendations in the earlier part of the Course on how the co-operation of the unconscious can be obtained by framing the suggestions in such a way that they will be approved both by the conscious and the unconscious mind.

One method of trance deepening is to write down a description of the experiences of sinking into a trance. The reader can call on his imagination to aid him here, describing his feelings in drifting off into sleep and incorporating some of the suggestions given below. This is an elaboration of what has been described as "Feed back Method." The reason for the reader compiling the material himself is that it will be his own experiences in his own words. The following are suggestions of the lines on which these self suggestions are to be prepared: "I am sitting in a chair— My body feels heavy—I am feeling very tired—I don't want to make any effort—of any kind—I feel drowsy and relaxed—This drowsiness is becoming deeper—My eyes are closed—I feel a lethargy stealing over me—My thoughts are becoming slower and. slower—It is just as though I were going to sleep—but I will be able to hear everything that goes on. My breathing is becoming slower, quieter and deeper. My whole system feels rested—My eyes feel very heavy—Emotionally I feel in a quiet, pleasant, contented state. I am physically and mentally completely relaxed—My legs are becoming heavier and heavier—My body, back and shoulders are relaxed—I have no desire to do anything—except rest—and let this drowsiness become deeper and deeper."

If the reader has difficulty in memorising, let him confine himself to short, simple repetitions. The reason for writing out the suggestions is to assist in remembering them. It is not necessary to be word perfect if the general theme expressed is one of deep relaxation. Let the reader select from the foregoing methods of induction the one from which he has experienced the best results. The next step is, when the maximum trance depth has been achieved, to employ the memorised material in the form of self-suggestions.

Take care that the clothing worn is loose-fitting and comfortable, and that you have bare feet, or comfortable shoes or slippers. It may be found helpful to have a light covering, a travelling rug or quilt, spread over you to ensure there are no draughts so that you are not cold. Pay particular attention to the temperature of the room and, if necessary, see that it is reasonably warm beforehand, and that it is not draughty. Arrange as far as you can that before the sessions there has been no abnormal expenditure of energy, that you have not been drawing deeply on your reserves of nervous energy. The purpose of this instruction is, if possible, to ensure that your level of nervous energy is not depleted or below normal, as this tends to increase tension. Some people find that to take off their shoes and place a hot water bottle at their feet is conducive to a trance, but by making these physical arrangements for comfort, the risk of going to sleep is increased.

A warm bath is very helpful, but with some people it will create the wrong conditions for trance induction. It is not possible to give specific instructions which will serve as a guide to everyone. Each individual reacts in a different way, in consequence of which the reader is advised to make a close and detailed study of his own reactions. By self observation he may possibly detect many small circumstances which will, without his knowledge, have been mildly disturbing him. For example, one student who practised his exercises in the late evening had failed to make any headway beyond light trance, and discovered that when he left off drinking tea in the evening the tension which he had previously experienced vanished immediately. The reader is recommended to study very closely all circumstances and actions which are likely to influence his attempts.

If the trance state goes too deep, the reader will only become aware of this when he wakes up. There is no record or evidence of anyone ever experiencing any inconvenience through self-induced trance. If, whilst carrying out the exercise, the reader enters a deep trance or falls fast asleep, he must, at the next session, induce a medium trance in which he does not allow himself to sink too deeply, and direct suggestions to prevent himself from losing control. These suggestions should be on the following lines: "I am sinking down into a trance, but I will not go to sleep, nor will I lose consciousness. I will be aware of any noises which go on outside, but they will not disturb me, and I will hear them all the while. The object of my practice and exercises is to implant suggestions in my unconscious mind and so that I shall be able to do this I must not lose consciousness or go to sleep."

It cannot be repeated too often that to effect alterations in oneself it is not necessary to hypnotise oneself. This course teaches how all the alterations which can be brought about in a self induced trance can be achieved through self suggestion.

The following exercise in disorientation is helpful in increasing depth of trance. It can be practised as a preliminary to a suggestion session.

Darkened Room. This preliminary exercise is to be carried out in total darkness. Complete darkness is employed in the training of insangomas (and many other mystics). In these cases the nature of the trance is different for it becomes possible to open the eyes without disturbing the trance (this is somnambulism). To reach this state a great deal of time and practice is necessary. It is difficult to maintain the delicate balance between either going off in unconsciousness and sleep or alternatively to become roused and alert. Practice this exercise in a completely darkened room. Experiment by walking about with a short stick in your hand and finding your way by touching objects with the end of the stick and very rapidly you will experience the sensation that you are "feeling" with the end of the stick. This is the beginning of a sensory extension. After you have carried out this experiment with both hands lie down with your eyes closed and place a forefinger *gently* on your eyelid and very, very gently apply pressure. If you move your finger when you touch certain spots you will probably see some flashes of light, possibly coloured lights. This is caused by pressure on the optic nerve and is to be carried out very gently indeed. Now remove your hands and mentally concentrate in the mind's eye, trying to re-visualise the flashes of light, without of course in any way touching your eyes. Keep your eyes closed while you are doing this. These vague shadowy half lights which are seen sometimes when the eyes are closed are the raw material out of which mental images are formed. They can also be formed by concentration. Turn your attention to try to build up images of the numeral one, see it like the Number 1 on a blackboard, that is as a white figure against a black background. When you have seen this, even if it is only vague, cancel it out and make the Number 2 appear. Cancel this and continue creating each number up to 10. The purpose of this exercise is not only of mental control but it also produces a dis-orientation and it will be found as a result of this and the following trance deepening exercise, that the depth of your trances will be improved.

For this trance deepening exercise lie down with your arms at your side and close your eyes. Do not try to create a trance but simply imagine a point moving round the outlines of your body. Begin at the crown of your head and imagine the point moving down the side of your head, tracing the outline of your ear, then down the side of your neck, along your shoulder down the outside of your arm until you come to the top of your little finger. Then trace the line in between your fingers around your thumb up the inside of your arm to your armpit, and then continue tracing the outline of your body until you have returned to the crown of your head. And continue with trance deepening suggestions.

CHAPTER THIRTEEN

OVERCOMING OBSTACLES

An obstacle in learning to hypnotise oneself can arise if the student has an exaggerated idea of what he imagines he will experience during the trance state. Not many people have the expectation of entering some strange mystical mental state and being wafted off to some indefinable realms, but sometimes preconceived ideas of what the trance state is, can hinder rather than help progress. If a student is trying to attain something which has no existence except in his own imagination this will obviously hinder his progress in the attainment of a real trance state.

Another obstacle can arise because students of self hypnosis very frequently underestimate the degree in which they have been affected in their practise sessions. It is an established fact that people tend to underestimate the depth of trance they have attained. Readers who are acquainted with text books on hypnosis will be well aware that frequently the subject's assessment of how far he had been hypnotised is quite incorrect. This is often due to an expectation of some strange experience and even when therapeutic benefits or post hypnotic suggestions are a demonstrable proof that hypnosis has been achieved, the subject will sometimes stubbornly maintain that he has not been hypnotised.

These two obstacles of undervaluation of progress and expectation of some mysterious experience during the trance state can be avoided by keeping an open mind in assessing and evaluating progress made in any particular session. This is achieved by avoiding negative comments such as "I am not doing this well," or "I'm not making progress."

The fact is that the trance state can vary vastly according to the mental and emotional attitude of the individual at the time he is carrying out a trance induction session. During the session he may be discharging muscular or emotional tensions and so appear to be restless and it may seem to him that he is not making progress, whereas in actual fact he is making real and positive steps towards achieving relaxation, emotional equilibrium and the trance state. On the other hand he may just relax and sink peacefully into a pleasant lethargic state. To avoid being influenced by the "ups and downs" which may be encountered in suggestion sessions it is wise to avoid any negative comments and concentrate on carrying out regular suggestion sessions.

In all cases the trance state is characterised by a sense of remoteness, but this does not mean losing consciousness.

Volitional control is never lost in the self hypnotic trance state. If self control is lost it is no longer self hypnosis for the individual drifts into a deeper trance which immediately turns into ordinary sleep from which he will wake in a normal manner. The length of time he sleeps will depend on how tired and comfortable he is and what external distractions are going on and what waking suggestions he has made to himself before beginning the suggestions session.

It is difficult to define mental and emotional states and conditions, but we can get some idea of what the trance state is if we examine a little more closely what happens when we go to sleep.

Actually it is not as though we were wide awake one moment and unconscious the next . . . though sometimes we appear to drop off to sleep suddenly. In reality, just before we lose consciousness, we pass rapidly through what in psychological language is called a hypnogogic condition, also in waking we pass through a somewhat similar condition described as hypnopompic. Both these states are hypnoidal trance states but they are both of such brief duration that normally during them, or subsequently on waking, we have no memory of them.

The self hypnotic trance state is induced by letting yourself sink beneath the surface of the mind or to withdraw awareness from the outside world into oneself until the focal point of awareness approaches the boundary which divides the conscious from the unconscious mind and to remain poised or suspended in this detached trance state.

The whole art is to remain mentally poised, not rising to the surface, for if we do we break the sense of detachment, nor sinking too deep for then we drift into oblivion. In this state, with practise, we learn to retain sufficient awareness to remain linked with the outside world. In this state or condition our Intellect and our Will lie ready at hand to be used if we wish to make the effort. If we remain quiescent in this suspended trance state we have achieved what Krishnamurti has called "Choiceless Awareness," and if we use self hypnosis positively we allow suggestions or possibly supplications, to pass through our minds. I say *allow*, for our suggestions are the voicing of our needs, our hopes, our wishes and desires arising from the depths of our being.

It sounds paradoxical to say that many people wishing to learn self hypnosis have already been, to all intents and purposes, hypnotised without their knowing it; that is to say that their real objective in learning self hypnosis is to *dehypnotise* themselves from some negative ideas or emotions.

Negative suggestions which have been put into a man's or woman's mind by someone else can ruin their lives, and frequently people are unaware that their shortcomings are due to the operation of damaging post hypnotic suggestions acquired as a result of a shock or accident. It has to be kept in mind that negative ideas and suggestions can be registered in the unconscious mind without the induction of a trance, and also that the victim may or may not consciously remember them.

A typical experience of this was related to me by a woman who, after her stepmother's death, had resigned herself to a lonely life in which work and worry were predominant. In her childhood her stepmother had unceasingly criticised her, telling her that she was stupid and ugly and that no man would ever look at her. When the stepmother died she was left alone, fearful and filled with feelings of inferiority. She had, to all intents and purposes, been brainwashed.

In her own quiet way she tried to help herself for she felt as though some invisible barrier was holding her back and preventing her from living an ordinary life. One night she went to a lecture on psychology where the lecturer carried out some experiments in hypnosis. Being a suggestible subject she responded well to his suggestions and was hypnotised. The hypnotist told her she would feel very confident and, for the first time in her life the woman experienced what it was like to feel free from fear and feelings of inferiority.

She went away from the lecture feeling that a new life was opening up for her. Unfortunately her new found confidence lasted only for a few days, but she knew from this experience that, even if it were only for a short time, it was possible to shed her fears, and she resolved to learn all she could about hypnosis. She attempted to get in touch with the lecturer but her letters were unanswered, so she began to read all she could about the subject.

She wrote to me telling me what had occurred at the lecture and asking me if I would teach her to hypnotise herself. I taught her how to create the trance state in herself and instructed her how she could remove the effects of past negative conditioning and build herself a new life.

This woman's experience was typical of the process of dehypnotisation . . . in fact it could be said she had experienced four different types of hypnotic conditioning.

The first was the negative conditioning of her stepmother constantly telling her that she was slow, stupid and awkward. Despite the fact that no formal trance had been induced the negative suggestions had been so effectively registered in the child's unconscious mind that, like a hypnotised subject, she had been acting out the stepmother's post hypnotic suggestions all her life. She had felt, acted and experienced exactly as her stepmother had said she would, and in fact had become the person her stepmother had said she would become.

The second phase was when the lecturer's hypnotic suggestions of confidence had temporarily cancelled out the stepmother's negative influence.

The third phase was when I hypnotised her in the course of teaching her how to hypnotise herself.

The fourth phase was when she began to use self hypnosis to remove all traces of the negative conditioning she had received in childhood, and for the first time to really express her own personality.

The purpose of relating this case history is to draw

attention to the fact that probably most hypnotic suggestions are concerned with removing damaging or negative ideas, emotions, attitudes or habits and DEHYPNO-TISING people from influences which prevent them from leading fuller lives.

As many readers will already know, or will have gathered from my former comments about using recordings to learn self hypnosis, if a subject is hypnotised by a hypnotist (or a hypnotic recording) and hypnotic suggestions are made to him that later he (the subject) will be able to hypnotise himself, then he will be able to do so. This sounds like a wonderful short cut, but there is rather more in learning self hypnosis than being hypnotised and having post hypnotic suggestions made to one by a hypnotist.

It is true that one can learn self hypnosis in this way but it is inadvisable to do so without first acquiring some knowledge of the subject. Self hypnosis is a potent power which, like most powers, can be misused. In the hands of someone who has no self knowledge, self hypnosis is like a learner driver in charge of a powerful racing car. I saw an example of this misuse when a man who was an excellent hypnotic subject had a very badly poisoned foot. He was a mechanic who had spilt some melted solder on his foot and had given himself hypnotic suggestions that his foot would not pain him and that he would forget all about it. He successfully blocked out the pain and by ignoring nature's warning had a badly poisoned foot. I am not suggesting that the average individual would be as imprudent as this, but those learning self hypnosis should learn how they can use and direct the power they are acquiring.

In learning self hypnosis there is a development of co-ordination between mental and emotional processes which is akin to the development of the body through physical exercise; the acquisition of psychological instead of physical skills. The ability to withdraw into oneself in even a light trance is not a kind of psychological trick but a skill which, like other skills, improves with practise.

There is no reason why a hypnotist's aid should not be called upon to help in learning self hypnosis, but it should be remembered that if the ability is acquired through the post hypnotic suggestions of someone else, the initiation (if I can call it that) should be followed by regular daily sessions to bed down the habit and make it one's own before the post hypnotic suggestions fade, which they will tend to do unless practice in trance induction is carried out for some weeks.

The soundest course to follow would be to practise on the lines set out in the foregoing pages and if, for some reason or other, progress seems slow and the help of a hypnotist is available, there is no reason why his help should not be called upon.

I have, as far as possible, avoided making personal references to myself, but I feel it would be helpful to mention that in acquiring my own knowledge of the subject I spent some nine years overseas in Africa and India, visiting many mystics, witch doctors, sadhus and indigenous healers who were practising what I am convinced were various forms of hypnosis. In India the techniques are known as moorchana shastrum or vashee karana vidya. In the Arab world it is known as Tanweem and in most places I visited I found versions of hypnosis or self hypnosis.

This strange psychological phenomena is not explained by giving it a name as did Dr. Braid when he christened it hypnosis any more than electricity or atomic energy is explained by naming them; we can see their manifestations but the hidden mystery eludes us.

I found during my travels that most healing methods demanded on the part of those who sought help, belief in a Saint, a God, a holy relic, an image or a shrine, and in many cases a trance state was experiencèd by devotees. All faiths bring about improvements in some of their followers . . . but it does appear that as man's critical faculty develops his ability to give himself up unreservedly in this simple act of faith diminishes. It seems that as man's reason develops it weakens his faith and, for a time, puts nothing in its place. This I believe is an inevitable stage in development, and I also believe we are now living in an age which is seeing the dawn of new Mental Sciences. Foremost amongst these and within the grasp of anyone who wishes to explore these new fields is self hypnosis. It is an uncommitted faith. . . it asks nothing except the courage to explore new methods and keep an open mind.

CONCLUSION

IN THIS LAST SECTION THERE ARE A NUMBER OF POINTS WHICH MAY BE FOUND HELPFUL AS ADVICE OR REMINDERS.

Do not be uneasy or doubtful about "coming to" or "waking up" from any of the states of consciousness which are induced. Before you begin exercises, estimate what time you have available—just think to yourself: "I've got half-an-hour to spend," (or whatever the period may be). Impress the thought on your mind, and carry on with your exercise. Although you have apparently pushed away the thought, there is a part of your mind which will prompt you when the period is nearing its end. If the conscious mind had forgotten the time your sub-conscious mind would remind you.

— — — — —

When practising your self suggestion sessions do not be uneasy about going into a very deep trance. If this did happen the experience is somewhat similar to that of dropping off to sleep. The deep trance state will turn into a normal sleep from which, after a brief rest, you will wake in a perfectly normal manner.

— — — — —

The most convenient times to employ self suggestion are immediately after waking, and just before going to sleep. Generally speaking, auto-suggestions are not so effective when energy level is low, though our impressionability to suggestions from others is increased. It is good practice to follow a regular routine, spending three or four minutes every morning and night on constructive suggestions.

If during your first few sessions you become aware of various tensions ... do not feel in any way disturbed. This is a part of the process of unwinding. Repressed tensions have to go somewhere, some subside and others discharge themselves when the will is switched off and you "let go." If a muscle twitches or you feel a vague restlessness, as far as you can disregard these tensions rising to the surface, think to yourself "I'm pleased to get rid of that," and carry on with your exercise. The tensions may continue to arise for a few sessions but will soon disappear.

— — — — —

It is essential to direct suggestions towards the removal of negative attitudes which have arisen as a result of reverses or disappointments. From day to day incorporate in your suggestions, varying ideas to the effect that your exercises will yield progressive benefits.

— — — — —

Never forget that pain and fatigue are nature's signals for attracting our attention. Suggestions should not be used to cancel out these signals before ascertaining their causes. Do not remove symptoms of pain or fatigue unless you are sure it is wise to do so. ALWAYS OBTAIN A MEDICAL OPINION REGARDING ANY SUSPICIOUS OR PERSISTENT PAIN OR SYMPTOM.

— — — — —

Repeat suggestions whilst fully awake. Repeat them as rapidly as possible. Tie twenty knots in a piece of string and carry this about with you in your pocket or handbag. This is a useful reminder to practice your suggestions, and by passing a knot between your finger and thumb each time a suggestion is made, it can be used to check the number of times the suggestions are repeated.

During self observation, you will have noticed that there are some sayings which seem to give strength and support. Make a note of any which appeal to you. It does not matter how simple, platitudinous or colloquial they may be, such as: "It's a good job I've got a sense of humour," or: "There are plenty of people worse off than I am," or: "I've been through worse troubles than this," or: "This can't go on forever." Simple statements of this nature have given people powerful aid when they desperately needed it. Though these suggestions are palliative in nature they have value as perspective correctors, and in sustaining morale.

The length of the suggestion sessions can be of comparatively short duration when progress has been made with the exercises. This is due to the fact that the time taken for getting into a suggestible state of mind is shortened, and experimentation is no longer necessary. Some people, once the habit of "letting go," or "putting oneself off," has been acquired, are able to put themselves into a medium depth of trance in a few seconds. When this stage has been arrived at, one or two minutes are ample for suggestion sessions. Until then, the major part of the time is spent in learning how to induce this stage of heightened suggestibility. This will account for approximately nine-tenths of the time which in the early stages, is taken up in studying the technique. At the beginning, practically the whole of the time is taken up by relaxation exercises, and very little self treatment is given, but once a trance or the detached state can be created, practically all the time is occupied in registering impressions.

As an exercise in auto-hypnosis and self suggestion, take advantage of the well-known fact that, by impressing on your mind the idea that you will wake at a certain hour the next morning, you are likely to do so. This is best carried out immediately before sleeping. The ability to successfully effect these projected orders grows with practice.

When making suggestions to yourself take your time, express them aloud or mentally. The thoughts must flood the whole mind to the exclusion of everything else. There must be no thinking, no analysing, no self-observation about whatever you are saying: no self-criticism. All the thinking and all the analysing should have been done beforehand. Make and accept the suggestions you are putting to yourself, with conviction. Give yourself up to the belief that what you are saying is so, in every respect. In the measure you are able to surrender yourself to these suggestions, your conviction will grow stronger.

Self Hypnotism or Autosuggestion, is a means to an end. The life of any individual should be lived, arranged and organised, in full waking consciousness. Self hypnotism and suggestion are only a means of building the habits necessary to live in a healthy, balanced manner.

If, when carrying out an exercise, for some reason you wish to suspend operations, do not hesitate or be irresolute. Decisively stop your exercise and postpone it as a definite act of will. This definite action on your part will prevent your being affected by negative suggestions, as you might be if the exercises continued in a desultory fashion, and deteriorated into a half-hearted attempt.

Having read through the whole of the work the reader is now advised if he has not already done so to commence practical work on the exercises. He is also advised, in addition to carrying out the exercises, to re-read the

Course at intervals, as each time it is read further information may be gained which was not apparent at earlier readings.

As the days pass devote what time you can to a routine of regular Suggestion Sessions ... Observing yourself ... Reflecting on any amendments or additions to the suggestions you are making ... and incorporating these in your next suggestion session. Changes will be observed. A life undergoing a transformation is often like a garden growing. The changes are sometimes slow and imperceptible ... sometimes dramatic and startling, but whether they are slow or rapid, improvements depend on individual cases. Stomach ulcers can be cured but the tissue changes take time. Hidden obstacles will come to light, self created difficulties may become apparent, but so also will the methods for dealing with these difficulties, methods of which the individual would never have consciously thought. It will soon be discovered that the unconscious mind has far greater wisdom than the conscious mind. If with sincerity we call on the unconscious mind, or the Unknown, it will soon be discovered that we are indeed invoking powers truly capable of performing miracles. The method of bringing into operation these powers is extremely simple—we must sincerely direct efforts to freeing within ourselves the mighty powers which are the source of all life. If, what we are trying to achieve, is for our good and in accord with the creative forces which work through all life, it will not be long before, through our co-operation with these forces, we are enjoying a harmonious way of life.

It should be borne in mind that unexpected circumstances may arise which will interfere with, or upset the arrangements you have planned for practice sessions. Should temporary setbacks of this nature be encountered, it must be remembered that you are no longer dealing with your difficulties with the simple outlook of one who believes that he must either be a success or a failure. But with the enlightened outlook of one who knows his limitations and is overcoming them by consciously choosing the suggestions which determine his attitude of mind and actions, and who is not letting chance and circumstances choose them for him. With this thought in mind, do temporary setbacks really matter ... so long as the goal is eventually reached?

In the beginning of this Course I said that anyone thrown on his own resources to overcome some problem or ailment, would, once he finds the way emerge from the ordeal far stronger than he was before.

Faith and belief sustain us in our hour of need, but because of the complexity of some of the problems with which we are faced today our faith needs reinforcing with understanding. Man is conquering the forces of nature in the outside world through his knowledge of the laws of nature, and in the same way many people are curing psychosomatic ills, resolving conflicts and developing their latent abilities through a knowledge of the laws which govern their own mental and emotional life.

We do not need to understand the nature of thought or emotion, any more than we need to know the nature of electricity, in order to direct and harness its power. In this Course is set out a system of redirecting and harnessing our mental and emotional energies, so that they may flow into their predestined channels and in this way we may achieve physical well being, and peace of mind.